Victoria Rey

The Fortune Cookie Cookbook

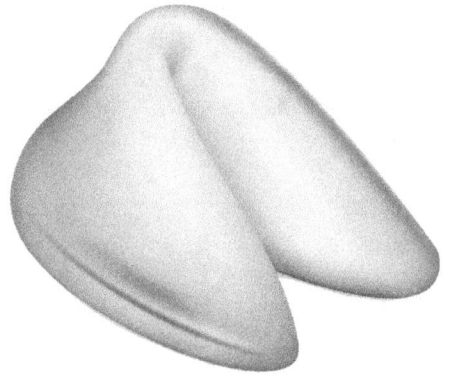

With History, Original Recipe and Variations, and More than 1300 Fortunes with their corresponding Lucky Numbers ready to cut out.

© All rights reserved. No part of this book may be reproduced in text or images by any means, without written permission.

1st Edition

© Calli Casa Editorial 2008

© Yhacar Trust, 2024

Text By Victoria Rey

General Supervision: Bernabé Pérez.

www.2GoodLuck.com

Calli Casa Editorial

Lake Elsinore, CA 92530

Origins of the Fortune Cookie

Despite their association with Chinese cuisine, fortune cookies actually originated in Japan, not China. They were first introduced to the United States by Japanese immigrants in the late 19th or early 20th century.

Early Versions: The early versions of fortune cookies in the United States were often made with a darker, more savory batter and contained more general aphorisms or proverbs rather than personalized fortunes.

Modern Fortune Cookies: Today, fortune cookies are typically made with a sweeter, lighter batter and contain individualized messages printed on small slips of paper. These messages can range from words of wisdom and encouragement to predictions about the future or humorous anecdotes.

Fortune Cookie Manufacturing: Most fortune cookies are produced in specialized factories using automated machinery. The batter is poured onto circular molds, baked, and then quickly folded around a slip of paper by a machine before it hardens.

Fortune Cookie Messages: Fortune cookie messages are carefully selected to be positive, uplifting, and often vague enough to apply to a wide range of situations. They may include words of wisdom, inspirational quotes, predictions about the future, or playful jokes.

Fortune Cookie Day: National Fortune Cookie Day is celebrated on July 20th in the United States. It's a day to enjoy fortune cookies and reflect on the messages they contain.

Fortune Cookie Controversies: Fortune cookies have occasionally sparked controversies, such as when some people found messages inside that were deemed offensive or inappropriate. However, most fortune cookies today strive to provide universally positive and inclusive messages.

Fortune Cookie Collecting: Some people collect fortune cookie messages as a hobby, seeking out unique or unusual fortunes to add to their collections. There are even online forums and communities dedicated to sharing and trading fortune cookie messages.

Fortune Cookie Variations: While the classic fortune cookie is made with a vanilla-flavored batter and contains a slip of paper with a message inside, there are many variations available today. Some fortune cookies are dipped in chocolate, flavored with different extracts, or even filled with non-traditional messages or prizes.

Cultural Impact: Fortune cookies have become a beloved part of Chinese cuisine in many parts of the world and are often served as a dessert or snack in Chinese restaurants. They also hold a special place in popular culture, appearing in movies, television shows, and even literature as symbols of luck, mystery, and fate.

These are just a few fascinating facts about fortune cookies! Whether you enjoy them for their sweet taste or the intrigue of their hidden messages, fortune cookies continue to captivate and delight people around the globe.

Recipe

Ingredients:

2 large egg whites

1/2 cup (100g) granulated sugar

1/4 cup (60ml) vegetable oil

1/2 teaspoon vanilla extract

1/2 cup (65g) all-purpose flour

Pinch of salt

2-4 tablespoons water

Cut the fortune slips from this book, as many as you need.

Variations: Use Jasmine tea instead of water to add an exotic flavor. Substitute half of the all-purpose flour for rice flour to add more crunch. Use almond extract instead of vanilla for a different flavor. Add a pinch of Cardamom for an extra kick. Or dip them into melted chocolate for a sumptuous experience.

Instructions:

Preheat Oven:

Preheat your oven to 350°F (175°C).

Line a baking sheet with parchment paper or a silicone baking mat.

Whisk Egg Whites:

In a mixing bowl, whisk the egg whites until frothy but not stiff.

Mix Wet Ingredients:

Add the granulated sugar, vegetable oil, and vanilla extract to the egg whites. Mix until well combined.

Add Dry Ingredients:

Gradually add the all-purpose flour and pinch of salt to the wet ingredients, mixing until a smooth batter forms.

Add Water:

Stir in the water until the batter becomes thin and smooth. The consistency should be similar to pancake batter.

Form Cookies:

Place tablespoons of batter onto the prepared baking sheet, spacing them about 3 inches apart. Use the back of a spoon or an offset spatula to spread the batter into circles about 4 inches in diameter.

Bake:

Bake the cookies in the preheated oven for 8-10 minutes, or until the edges are lightly golden brown.

Add Fortunes:

Working quickly while the cookies are still hot and flexible, place a fortune in the center of each cookie. Use a spatula to fold the cookie in half, then gently bend the folded edge over the rim of a glass or cup to create the classic fortune cookie shape. Repeat with the remaining cookies.

Cool:

Transfer the formed cookies to a wire rack to cool completely. As they cool, they will harden into the crisp texture of fortune cookies.

Enjoy:

Once cooled, your fortune cookies are ready to enjoy! Serve them as a fun and unique dessert or snack, and don't forget to share the fortunes with your friends and family.

Storage:

Store any leftover fortune cookies in an airtight container at room temperature for up to one week. Make sure to place a small piece of parchment paper between each cookie to prevent them from sticking together.

Enjoy making and sharing these homemade fortune cookies!

A bird in the hand is safer than one overhead.	A fresh start will put you on your way.
A bird in your hand is worth more than 100 in the forest.	A friend in need will be out of your way soon.
A book holds a house of gold.	A friend is a present you give yourself.
A book is like a garden carried in the pocket.	A friend's success will benefit you.
A close friend reveals a hidden talent.	A gambler not only loses what he has, but also loses what he doesn't have.
A closed mind is like a closed book; just a block of wood.	A gathering of friends brings you lots of luck this evening.
A dog won't forsake his master because of his poverty; a son never deserts his mother for her homely appearance.	A good deed done today is repaid in double tomorrow.
A dream will present the key to a hidden truth.	A good friendship is often more important than a passionate romance.
A dubious friend may be an enemy in camouflage.	A good home is happiness.
A faithful friend is a strong defense.	A great man never ignores the simplicity of a child.
A fall into a ditch makes you wiser.	A heart full of gratitude is a magnet for miracles.
A fall into a ditch will make you wiser.	A huge fortune at home is not as good as money in use.
A financial investment will yield returns beyond your hopes.	A journey of a thousand miles begins with a single step. Start stepping!

11-24-27-57-62 + 01	19-26-38-58-59 + 07
08-28-29-58-67 + 01	27-40-48-50-67 + 07
06-39-44-55-66 + 02	04-28-29-56-59 + 07
02-14-19-47-56 + 02	12-17-22-43-66 + 08
01-25-33-47-60 + 02	08-09-28-42-62 + 08
16-22-33-38-52 + 03	20-24-39-45-51 + 09
11-23-50-63-69 + 03	13-22-29-68-69 + 10
07-15-34-44-63 + 03	21-24-47-50-59 + 10
11-35-53-59-65 + 03	21-24-47-50-59 + 10
07-08-15-21-51 + 04	10-11-39-54-62 + 10
37-39-40-41-51 + 05	02-45-46-50-69 + 11
10-17-22-26-46 + 06	13-23-50-53-54 + 11
23-34-40-54-61 + 07	01-15-33-65-69 + 11

A kind word can change someone's entire day. Spread kindness like confetti!	A romantic evening awaits you tonight.
A lifetime of happiness is ahead of you.	A secret admirer will soon appear.
A light heart carries you through all the hard times.	A secret admirer will soon send you a sign of affection.
A man must insult himself before others will.	A ship in a harbor is safe, but that is not what ships are built for.
A needle is sharp only on one end.	A single kind word will keep one warm for years.
A new adventure awaits you this weekend.	A smile is the shortest distance between two people. Share yours often!
A new environment makes all the difference in the world.	A smile is your personal welcome mat.
A new idea could be profitable.	A soft voice may be very persuasive.
A new perspective will come with the New Year.	A surprise treat awaits you.
A new sense of clarity is coming into your life.	A true friend walks in when the rest of the world walks out.
A person of words and not deeds is like a garden full of weeds.	A truly rich life contains love and art in abundance.
A quiet evening with friends is the best tonic for a long day.	A vacation by the sea is in store for you.
A romantic evening at home is the best way to relax.	A well-directed imagination is the source of great deeds.

12-32-34-37-40 + 11

01-18-52-65-67 + 11

03-28-34-43-57 + 12

08-17-43-57-69 + 13

03-12-43-47-63 + 13

19-21-27-48-50 + 13

17-35-41-54-62 + 14

26-47-49-62-67 + 15

22-27-54-67-69 + 15

04-16-19-37-59 + 16

13-39-46-54-66 + 16

16-50-53-67-69 + 18

02-07-18-26-61 + 18

14-26-29-40-61 + 19

14-30-32-57-63 + 19

07-51-55-56-66 + 20

08-17-40-56-62 + 20

45-46-54-58-69 + 21

05-26-40-53-65 + 21

25-27-32-44-47 + 21

03-18-37-43-45 + 22

04-30-47-54-57 + 22

06-11-13-19-43 + 23

11-36-56-60-65 + 24

17-22-28-32-49 + 25

40-44-67-8-52+11

Acceptance of what you can't change is the key to inner peace.	Aim high, but remember to enjoy the climb.
Act with courage, for even the smallest act of bravery can ignite great change.	Aim not for perfection, but for progress. Every step forward counts.
Act with intention, and the universe will conspire to make it happen.	All happiness is in the mind.
Act with kindness, speak with love, and the universe will respond in kind.	All of your troubles will go away very quickly.
Advancement will come with hard work.	All the answers you need are right there in front of you!
Adventure awaits around every corner. Embrace the unknown!	All the effort you are making will ultimately pay off.
Adventure awaits those who dare to seek it with an open heart.	All the news you receive will be positive and uplifting.
Adventure is calling. Answer with courage and curiosity.	All the preparation you've done will finally pay off!
Adventure is out there, but sometimes the greatest journey is within.	All the troubles you have will pass away very quickly.
Adversity introduces a person to themselves. Embrace the lessons it brings.	All will go well with your new project.
Advice, when most needed, is least heeded.	All your hard work will soon pay off.
Age can never hope to win you while your heart is young.	All your hard work will soon pay off. Keep pushing forward!
Aim for the moon. Even if you miss, you'll land among the stars.	Allow yourself to be a beginner; every master was once a beginner.

56-59-42-41-52+15

4-60-14-17-54+3

6-9-34-66-68+9

44-20-27-59-40+8

43-27-56-60-39+1

41-34-32-55-22+15

30-62-21-27-69+8

6-26-10-65-69+24

55-40-4-66-53+25

37-33-38-63-49+22

20-38-41-15-34+4

41-30-23-62-36+5

33-59-22-56-3+16

33-60-46-41-25+9

66-27-45-5-57+18

55-3-39-61-33+8

35-39-37-67-5+9

43-19-37-18-14+20

18-10-62-23-53+16

55-27-64-46-4+5

6-27-58-57-4+20

1-41-19-20-29+7

45-67-61-69-17+20

20-24-18-26-50+20

52-38-28-49-68+19

19-44-2-15-34+10

Allow yourself to dream big, for dreams are the seeds of reality.	An unexpected event will bring you riches.
Although it feels like a roller coaster now, life will calm down.	An unexpected relationship will become permanent.
Always bathe in the river of love.	Anger is a condition in which the tongue works faster than the mind.
Always choose love, for it is the most powerful force in the universe.	Answer just what your heart prompts you.
Always remember that you are unique. Just like everyone else.	Any doubts you may have will disappear early this month
Always remember: the best is yet to come.	Appearances can be deceiving. Remember endurance makes gold.
Always trust your intuition; it's your inner compass guiding you.	Apply yourself to the basics and progress will follow.
Amidst challenges, remember: you are stronger than you realize.	Appreciate the beauty in simplicity; life's true treasures often lie in the little things.
Among the lucky, you are the chosen one.	Appreciate the journey as much as the destination; both hold value.
An admirer is too shy to greet you.	Appreciate the small moments—they often hold the greatest joy.
An enjoyable vacation is awaiting you.	As you sow, so shall you reap. Plant seeds of kindness and watch them bloom.
An inch of time is an inch of gold.	Ask a friend to join you on your next voyage.
An open heart is an invitation to miracles. Keep yours open.	Aspire to inspire before you expire.

58-59-27-16-40+18   51-16-52-12-35+21

17-25-68-37-44+1   8-24-59-27-8+22

24-12-57-47-58+4   31-40-4-25-18+3

25-69-2-39-50+16   49-66-54-10-1+21

56-25-46-13-44+23   49-55-12-37-14+4

17-51-55-61-10+10   21-16-49-34-11+6

62-11-15-51-54+8   1-53-24-35-7+15

63-57-6-5-19+14   43-53-59-14-9+14

35-20-52-30-48+2   16-14-24-59-40+8

37-3-17-62-65+5   50-42-69-47-17+21

31-51-24-48-52+21   44-21-66-64-25+11

53-42-28-11-69+14   16-14-49-69-31+14

20-57-45-55-5+25   56-27-8-6-5+8

Attract what you expect, reflect what you desire, become what you respect.	Be the change you wish to see in the world. Start within.
Avoid senseless contradictions with others.	Be the light in someone's darkness; your kindness matters.
Balance is the key to a harmonious life; find your equilibrium.	Beauty in its various forms appeals to you.
Balance your ambitions with moments of stillness; both are essential.	Beauty surrounds you; take a moment to appreciate it.
Be bold in your pursuits, and success will follow.	Because you demand more from yourself, others respect you deeply.
Be brave enough to listen to the whispers of your heart.	Begin each day with a grateful heart and end it with contentment.
Be careful not to overspend.	Believe in miracles, for they happen every day in unexpected ways.
Be curious, for curiosity leads to discovery and growth.	Believe in the beauty of your dreams; they are your guiding stars.
Be fearless in the pursuit of what sets your soul on fire.	Believe in the magic of new beginnings; every sunrise brings opportunity.
Be gentle with yourself; you're doing the best you can.	Believe in the power of positive thinking; it shapes your reality.
Be open to receiving the blessings that flow into your life.	Believe in the power of your dreams; they are the blueprints of your destiny.
Be patient; the universe unfolds its wonders in its own time.	Believe in your ability to overcome any obstacle; resilience is your superpower.
Be present in each moment; life's greatest joys are found in the now.	Believe in your innate worthiness; you are enough, just as you are.

3-7-57-14-32+23   48-9-25-68-42+17

21-22-38-53-9+21   47-51-44-57-65+22

19-6-48-41-33+8   16-48-68-53-10+13

9-44-41-29-69+11   31-5-4-11-10+23

33-62-47-18-63+16   68-11-54-7-17+23

56-24-48-60-41+10   36-34-41-61-22+8

23-9-55-11-37+14   62-40-49-30-5+16

11-20-9-69-21+8   24-39-13-49-64+4

64-27-6-61-54+25   69-2-43-33-59+22

11-13-44-66-18+9   45-57-33-56-15+15

45-15-29-27-36+11   33-59-12-47-57+16

40-38-65-47-68+18   37-20-30-22-63+6

68-47-69-26-63+24   62-37-48-30-55+6

Believe in yourself, and anything is possible.	Cast your dreams into the universe like seeds in fertile soil; watch them grow into reality.
Believe that every ending is a new beginning in disguise.	Cast your worries to the wind; they only weigh down your spirit.
Believe that every setback is a setup for a comeback.	Celebrate your uniqueness; it's what makes you shine.
Better caution at first than tears afterwards. A long journey awaits you.	Challenge yourself to grow beyond your comfort zone; that's where true magic happens.
Better to light a candle than to curse the darkness.	Change is happening in your life, so go with the flow!
Blessings often come disguised as challenges. Embrace them.	Channel your energy into something positive.
Blossom where you are planted, for greatness lies within you.	Chase your passions with unwavering determination; success will follow.
Breathe deeply and let go of worries; peace is within reach.	Cherish the journey as much as the destination; each step is a part of your story.
Breathe deeply and trust the journey; you are exactly where you need to be.	Cherish the present moment, for it holds the key to happiness.
Brighter days are ahead; keep your eyes on the horizon.	Choose forgiveness over resentment; it's the path to inner peace.
Build bridges with kindness, for they connect hearts and souls.	Choose happiness as a daily practice, not a distant destination.
Capture moments of joy like fireflies in a jar; savor their glow during darker times.	Choose joy as your compass; it will guide you through life's storms.
Carve your own path in life; the road less traveled often leads to extraordinary destinations.	Choose kindness in all that you do; it's the language of the heart.

49-37-32-63-23+25

52-62-44-32-33+15

57-35-54-49-51+7

38-29-65-45-14+10

40-2-14-11-25+15

39-42-62-10-30+18

2-13-6-4-40+10

17-45-5-57-47+2

48-64-54-37-38+23

14-61-3-17-39+3

7-30-37-45-67+14

34-69-20-35-30+15

45-17-47-68-8+6

4-2-26-14-25+10

64-53-7-63-50+11

65-3-56-25-5+15

10-20-23-14-17+16

53-11-63-45-20+16

39-53-28-30-22+10

50-35-16-24-48+6

57-59-69-40-16+8

9-35-68-67-59+9

69-63-65-67-27+9

5-69-35-56-63+7

54-52-7-19-35+14

17-2-26-43-10+5

Choose love as your guiding light; it has the power to transform the world.	Cultivate a spirit of adventure; life's greatest treasures lie off the beaten path.
Clarity comes to those who seek it with an open mind and heart.	Cultivate a spirit of curiosity; life is an endless adventure of discovery.
Common sense is not so common.	Cultivate an attitude of gratitude, and watch your blessings multiply.
Competence like yours is underrated.	Cultivate compassion for yourself and others; it's the true measure of strength.
Congratulations! You are on your way.	Cultivate gratitude, and abundance will follow.
Connect with others authentically; meaningful relationships enrich the soul.	Cultivate inner peace amidst life's chaos; it's a sanctuary for the soul.
Consider gain and loss, but never be greedy and everything will be all right.	Cultivate patience; the seeds you plant today will blossom in due time.
Consolidate business projects in the near future.	Cultivate resilience in the face of adversity; you are stronger than you know.
Courageously face your fears; they hold the keys to your growth.	Dance to the rhythm of your heart's desires; it's the music of your soul.
Courageously pursue your dreams; they are your destiny waiting to unfold.	Dare to be compassionate; it's the language of the heart that heals wounds.
Create a life that feels good on the inside, not just one that looks good on the outside.	Dare to be different; it's what makes you extraordinary.
Create a vision for your life and take bold steps towards its realization.	Dare to be grateful for life's blessings; gratitude opens doors to abundance.
Create your own sunshine on cloudy days; positivity is contagious.	Dare to be patient; the universe unfolds its wonders in perfect timing.

29-25-37-18-46+18   52-44-26-22-57+12

42-39-53-18-12+13   8-9-41-14-45+5

1-25-30-66-55+22   63-67-15-9-63+2

7-50-68-15-28+7   54-28-5-37-21+11

57-49-15-29-12+17   13-55-69-60-33+1

15-40-27-52-29+18   37-52-31-40-33+3

67-61-58-42-66+2   26-57-69-12-9+10

23-19-42-13-27+4   28-26-21-30-16+20

50-60-11-13-30+11   15-12-65-42-68+5

38-69-14-39-37+22   28-14-32-10-60+25

19-25-26-5-47+13   49-40-32-41-69+12

59-43-63-13-21+7   8-7-55-42-5+23

23-37-59-2-3+9   69-8-14-36-62+20

Dare to be present in each moment; life's beauty unfolds in the now.	Dare to seek wisdom in silence; the answers you seek lie within.
Dare to be the architect of your destiny; your choices shape your future.	Dare to speak your truth; your voice has the power to inspire and uplift.
Dare to be the change you wish to see in the world; your actions matter.	Dare to stand tall in the face of adversity; resilience is your greatest strength.
Dare to be the light in someone's darkness; your kindness can change lives.	Dedicate yourself with a calm mind to the task at hand.
Dare to be vulnerable; it's the birthplace of authenticity and connection.	Delight in the simple pleasures of life; they are the true treasures.
Dare to be yourself; you are enough, just as you are.	Diligence is the mother of good fortune.
Dare to believe in yourself; you are capable of more than you imagine.	Disbelief destroys the magic.
Dare to dream boldly; your imagination knows no limits.	Discover the beauty in imperfection; it's what makes life uniquely beautiful.
Dare to embrace failure as a stepping stone to success.	Discover the magic within you; it's the key to unlocking your potential.
Dare to explore the unknown; adventure awaits beyond the horizon.	Distance yourself from the vain.
Dare to forgive; it liberates the soul and heals the heart.	Dive deep into your soul; therein lies the wisdom you seek.
Dare to let go of what no longer serves you; liberation follows surrender.	Dive into each moment with passion and purpose; life is meant to be lived fully.
Dare to love fiercely; it's the most powerful force in the universe.	Dive into the depths of your soul; therein lies the source of your power.

42-1-44-45-43+3   54-64-42-6-39+8

6-34-57-54-15+6   62-48-12-67-15+18

9-61-25-13-18+25   61-50-64-17-42+11

64-3-6-59-39+17   28-14-11-5-23+4

37-47-35-20-22+11   18-3-20-35-28+2

53-35-21-20-62+21   59-12-62-34-14+5

31-66-40-2-11+13   8-23-60-16-19+13

48-29-64-2-36+25   57-18-36-61-60+15

20-48-10-30-29+9   38-49-22-43-36+5

32-31-41-63-40+4   44-8-57-38-56+25

43-36-22-49-36+21   37-18-11-5-66+10

39-12-49-32-7+11   48-29-59-16-49+21

50-58-38-40-1+25   16-1-60-31-36+5

Dive into the ocean of possibility; your dreams await on the other shore.	Each obstacle on your path is becoming the gateway to a new life!
Do not be afraid to take a big step.	Embrace change as a doorway to new opportunities.
Do not be intimidated by the eloquence of others.	Embrace each day with gratitude, for it holds the promise of new beginnings.
Do not be too eager to let others use your money.	Embrace the beauty of diversity; it enriches the tapestry of life.
Do not make extra work for yourself.	Embrace the beauty of imperfection; it adds depth to your story.
Do not mistake temptation for opportunity.	Embrace the challenges that come your way; they strengthen your spirit.
Do what you can, money will follow.	Embrace the journey of self-discovery; it leads to profound growth.
Don't behave with bad manners.	Embrace the lessons of the past; they are stepping stones to a brighter future.
Don't confuse recklessness with confidence.	Embrace the power of empathy; it fosters deeper connections with others.
Don't judge based on appearances.	Embrace the power of forgiveness; it liberates the soul and heals the heart.
Dream big, but remember to take small steps; progress is the key to success.	Embrace the power of imagination; it fuels your dreams and aspirations.
Dream different dreams while on the same bed.	Embrace the power of positive thinking; it shapes your reality.
Dream without limits; the universe conspires to make your dreams a reality.	Embrace the present moment fully; it's where life's magic unfolds.

33-1-22-38-23+12					47-13-37-66-69+2

13-35-59-22-32+22					64-37-60-36-27+2

40-52-32-45-44+14					62-43-55-47-42+16

64-53-34-27-31+2					10-25-45-46-16+17

53-46-47-58-64+24					54-27-14-53-29+23

3-30-43-5-15+21					56-42-49-40-69+11

4-51-53-16-54+6					4-2-52-44-7+4

14-4-53-41-4+24					5-63-64-21-1+5

65-31-6-43-22+6					67-40-35-32-34+24

26-14-17-51-53+14					11-10-1-35-21+20

14-18-17-69-60+17					13-22-6-47-15+17

64-59-12-31-58+17					34-15-53-1-57+22

66-6-3-59-2+20					23-49-37-17-56+18

Embrace the rhythm of life; sometimes you need to dance to your own beat.	Every ending is a new beginning in disguise; embrace change with an open heart.
Embrace the silence; within it, you may find the answers you seek.	Every flower blooms in its own sweet time.
Embrace the unknown with courage and curiosity; it holds infinite possibilities.	Every journey begins with a single step; have faith and keep moving forward.
Embrace your fears with courage; they are opportunities for bravery.	Every journey is unique; embrace the twists and turns as part of your adventure.
Embrace your inner strength; you are capable of overcoming any obstacle.	Every moment is a gift; cherish the present and create lasting memories.
Embrace your uniqueness; it's what makes you truly extraordinary.	Every person is the architect of their own fortune.
Emulate what you admire in your parents.	Every seed you plant of kindness blossoms into a garden of love.
Emulate what you respect in your friends.	Every setback is a setup for a comeback; resilience is your greatest asset.
Enjoy what you have! Never mind fame and power.	Every smile you share lights up the world; spread joy wherever you go.
Even a small gift could mean so much to someone today.	Every storm eventually passes, revealing clear skies once again.
Every act of kindness ripples outward, creating a wave of positivity.	Every sunrise brings a new beginning; greet each day with optimism.
Every challenge you face is an opportunity for growth and transformation.	Every truly great accomplishment is at first impossible.
Every dream you dare to dream is a glimpse into your infinite potential.	Everyone around you is rooting for you. Don't give up!

28-59-57-65-49+8   63-66-29-27-11+22

52-12-26-1-46+15   11-58-37-19-56+8

9-37-33-43-50+16   38-20-53-35-32+25

54-37-8-4-20+12   35-42-63-32-17+23

50-6-44-38-56+19   32-6-9-41-49+12

16-33-51-1-19+10   13-63-55-42-23+16

14-39-41-51-53+17   16-65-51-42-3+17

55-18-38-44-29+19   4-18-65-39-35+14

49-41-3-54-4+5   31-29-69-16-61+18

35-2-17-63-11+13   34-68-21-41-61+19

6-55-11-12-29+23   53-10-40-49-61+3

17-14-29-37-50+24   50-40-37-51-5+25

40-69-54-58-22+1   5-68-17-61-55+6

Everyone has the right to choose one's own lifestyle.	Feed your soul with laughter and love; they are the fuel of happiness.
Everyone sees what you appear to be; some realize what you are; few realize who you are.	Fight poison with poison.
Everything has its beauty but not everyone sees it.	Financial hardship in your life is coming to an end. Enjoy!
Everywhere you choose to go, friendly faces will greet you.	Find beauty in every moment, for life is a masterpiece in the making.
Explore the world with wonder and curiosity; adventure awaits at every turn.	Find joy in the journey, for it is where life's true magic resides.
Explore your own world by working together with your friends.	Find peace in the present moment; it's where true contentment resides.
Face each challenge with resilience; you are stronger than you know.	Find release from your cares and have a good time.
Face your fears with bravery; they are stepping stones to your growth.	Find solace in solitude; it's where you reconnect with your true self.
Failure is not an option; it is just a nagging possibility that helps one stay focused.	Find strength in adversity; it reveals the depth of your resilience.
Failure is the mother of success.	Flattery will go far tonight.
Fear less, live more; embrace life with fearless enthusiasm.	Flaws don't matter; who is without a flaw?
Fear not the unknown; it holds the keys to your greatest discoveries.	Flow with the rhythm of life; embrace its ebbs and flows with grace.
Feed your mind with knowledge; it's the key to unlocking your potential.	Focus on the journey as much as the destination; both hold value.

14-10-12-54-61+11   11-21-17-1-65+14

48-62-35-51-46+9   54-28-46-38-18+11

2-58-52-60-4+2   17-48-51-12-69+18

68-49-16-19-31+6   16-44-47-52-19+17

3-59-6-5-8+3   11-47-20-14-16+10

18-51-64-32-68+24   27-5-15-41-33+18

26-1-50-24-61+9   26-21-54-35-59+2

17-15-35-56-24+10   5-15-14-21-52+21

39-6-19-53-25+21   18-22-36-44-54+10

61-44-5-42-48+2   7-26-33-34-36+2

4-48-8-21-31+1   9-61-15-1-40+13

12-34-63-2-40+23   62-49-66-63-30+11

8-38-27-10-38+11   54-32-23-4-17+8

Focus on the present moment; it's where your power lies.	Fortune smiles upon those who believe in the beauty of their dreams.
Focus on what you can control; let go of what you cannot.	Foster a spirit of cooperation and collaboration; together, we thrive.
Follow the path of kindness; it leads to a world of compassion and love.	Foster gratitude in your heart; it transforms ordinary moments into blessings.
Follow the whispers of your intuition; they lead to extraordinary places.	Free speech carries with it freedom to listen.
Follow your heart; it knows the way to your true desires.	Fuel your dreams with determination; they are the seeds of your success.
Follow your passions with unwavering dedication; they lead to fulfillment.	Fulfillment comes from within; seek it in the depths of your soul.
Fool me once, shame on you; fool me twice, shame on me.	Garner strength from within; you are capable of overcoming any obstacle.
Forge ahead with confidence; you are capable of achieving greatness.	Gather courage from within; it's the fuel that propels you towards greatness.
Forge ahead with determination; your dreams are worth the journey.	Gather wisdom from life's experiences; they are the teachers on your journey.
Forge deep connections with others; they enrich the tapestry of your life.	Generosity and perfection are your everlasting goal.
Forge your own path in life; your uniqueness is your greatest strength.	Genius is one percent inspiration and ninety-nine percent, perspiration.
Fortune favors the bold; take courageous steps towards your dreams.	Get your mind set and confidence will lead you on.
Fortune favors those who dare to dream big and work hard.	Give voice to your dreams; they are the song of your soul waiting to be sung.

34-6-32-54-22+10   61-21-43-68-38+19

12-56-13-62-36+7   54-57-17-12-15+2

11-65-37-62-64+23   28-64-34-15-1+9

36-41-63-13-52+24   63-52-50-22-40+10

57-41-16-51-31+25   9-19-41-50-51+6

36-66-59-52-23+19   40-6-67-8-57+12

48-8-17-28-39+24   21-66-49-26-48+12

69-50-56-27-55+23   7-23-33-55-38+4

26-55-49-19-29+1   56-62-29-68-27+20

33-42-39-49-54+3   16-55-65-7-68+8

7-41-16-67-1+23   19-10-68-21-20+18

23-62-27-38-66+6   7-21-69-54-63+22

56-24-59-27-17+20   1-7-24-49-58+7

Give without expecting anything in return; generosity is its own reward.	Good advice will be given to you.
Give yourself permission to rest; it's essential for rejuvenating the soul.	Good beginning is half done.
Give yourself the gift of forgiveness; it sets you free from the past.	Good cloths open many doors. Go shopping.
Giving your son a skill is better than giving him one thousand pieces of gold.	Good health will be yours for a long time.
Gladden the hearts of others with acts of kindness; it's a gift that keeps on giving.	Good luck seldom comes in pairs, but bad things never occur alone.
Glide through life with grace and gratitude; it's a recipe for happiness.	Good Luck will be bestowed upon you. You will get what your heart desires.
Glimpse the beauty in every soul you meet; it enriches your own spirit.	Good news is just life's way of keeping you off balance.
Glow with the inner light of confidence; it illuminates your path to success.	Good things are coming to you soon.
Glow with the warmth of compassion; it heals wounds and nurtures hearts.	Good things come to those who believe, better things come to those who are patient, and the best things come to those who don't give up.
Go beyond your comfort zone; adventure and growth await in uncharted territory.	Good to begin well, better to end well.
Go confidently in the direction of your dreams; success awaits your arrival.	Good words are like a string of pearls.
Go where your heart leads you; it knows the way to your true happiness.	Gracefully navigate life's twists and turns; resilience is your guiding light.
Good advice jars the ear.	Grasp each moment with mindfulness; it's the essence of living fully.

45-13-36-68-22+4			47-38-9-65-59+7

53-10-56-17-66+4			1-37-2-10-60+8

36-55-61-21-51+16			45-3-9-26-51+14

61-33-11-27-15+17			22-68-11-69-44+11

7-22-41-66-14+5			26-57-40-65-43+15

16-63-9-68-20+25			32-20-59-40-14+13

51-40-29-32-33+22			55-39-15-56-49+7

54-64-21-46-20+1			22-48-59-56-11+15

46-38-65-51-48+24			55-15-39-37-68+7

13-49-68-14-5+9			6-59-28-16-55+22

51-3-67-7-14+11			32-1-48-15-16+12

5-4-48-43-53+15			52-2-68-60-63+19

61-6-7-8-12+16			69-2-50-26-51+1

Grasp every opportunity that comes your way; they are stepping stones to success.	Guard yourself against evil temptations.
Grasp opportunities to mold the future.	Guide your actions with integrity; it's the compass that leads to success.
Grasp the power of the present moment; it's where life's magic unfolds.	Guide your thoughts towards positivity; they shape your reality.
Gratitude unlocks the fullness of life; cherish the blessings around you.	Happier days are definitely ahead for you, your struggles have ended.
Gravitate towards positivity; it's a magnet for abundance and joy.	Happiness begins with facing life with a smile and a wink.
Gravitate towards the beauty in life; it's everywhere, waiting to be discovered.	Harbor no regrets; every experience has shaped the person you are today.
Great acts of kindness will befall you in the coming months.	Harmonize with nature; it restores balance and peace to the soul.
Greater success is in the days ahead.	Harmonize your mind, body, and spirit; balance is the key to well-being.
Greet each challenge with determination and resilience; victory is within reach.	Harness the energy of positivity; it attracts abundance into your life.
Greet each day with a smile; it's the key to a bright and joyful day.	Harness the power of imagination; it's the gateway to endless possibilities.
Grow through what you go through; every challenge is an opportunity for growth.	Harness the power of your dreams; they are the seeds of your future.
Grow your mind with knowledge; it's the key to unlocking new possibilities.	Haste does not bring success.
Guard your dreams with determination; they are the blueprints of your destiny.	Have a mouth as sharp as a dagger but a heart as soft as tofu.

60-66-40-33-15+22					3-64-47-41-52+7

69-50-9-34-61+8					37-55-12-64-40+17

44-20-12-46-37+17					15-9-4-19-69+5

69-50-56-28-25+23					9-28-22-69-11+10

40-27-67-45-57+19					61-36-26-57-8+23

26-61-46-28-22+15					51-4-42-22-16+18

61-27-54-69-36+19					34-6-44-27-28+14

51-10-50-34-40+18					26-54-25-3-12+23

21-63-48-50-28+13					42-32-61-9-1+20

14-67-22-36-49+1					66-20-40-65-1+1

27-35-29-40-30+13					50-12-8-27-64+7

6-39-42-8-16+9					68-46-18-56-4+24

38-25-6-16-33+4					69-5-41-49-37+8

Have faith in your abilities; you are more capable than you realize.	Hear you forget; see and you remember; do and you understand.
Have one's ears pierced only before the wedding ceremony starts.	Help others find their light; together, we illuminate the world.
He who expects no gratitude shall never be disappointed.	Help others rise; their success lifts us all higher.
He who has good health is young.	Help others without expecting anything in return; kindness is its own reward.
He who hurries can not walk with dignity.	Hold fast to your dreams; they are the blueprints of your destiny.
He who knows he has enough is rich.	Hold on to hope; it's the light that guides you through the darkest nights.
He who loves you will follow you.	Hold onto faith; it's the anchor that keeps you steady in life's storms.
He who never made a mistake, never made a discovery.	Hold onto gratitude; it's the key that unlocks the fullness of life.
He who seeks will find.	Hold onto joy; it's the elixir that nourishes the soul.
He who smiles in crisis has found someone to blame.	Hold onto love; it's the most powerful force in the universe.
He who throws dirt loses ground.	Hold onto optimism; it's the fuel that propels you towards your goals.
He who waits a great deal of time to do something will never do anything.	Hold onto resilience; it's the strength that carries you through adversity.
Heal old wounds with forgiveness; it's the balm that soothes the heart.	Hold space for silence; within it, lies the wisdom you seek.

43-15-6-22-2+9				32-22-60-16-8+23

42-35-37-6-61+4			24-19-14-28-10+21

47-29-69-6-11+17			53-40-65-33-23+11

12-55-28-27-2+2			13-51-61-41-31+4

39-18-16-38-43+2			40-66-55-1-69+21

68-41-65-7-36+13			36-11-68-51-35+7

62-20-26-46-48+1			54-58-55-25-42+9

32-43-21-24-67+25			31-28-45-1-30+1

21-44-43-40-49+8			47-22-48-15-19+16

54-21-38-69-17+16			42-69-54-67-10+11

4-50-34-28-23+22			12-10-15-22-26+23

12-34-68-18-23+19			56-64-17-61-55+10

30-36-29-8-67+25			32-35-67-13-12+21

Hone your skills with diligence; mastery is a journey, not a destination.	If a son is uneducated, his dad is to blame.
Hone your talents with dedication; they are the keys to unlocking your potential.	If a true sense of value is to be yours it must come through service.
Honor the bonds of friendship; they are the threads that weave our lives together.	If certainty were truth, we would never be wrong.
Honor the diversity of life; it enriches the tapestry of our world.	If you are willing to admit your faults, you have one less fault to admit.
Honor the journey of self-discovery; it leads to inner peace and fulfillment.	If you do not study hard when young, you'll end up bewailing your failures as you grow up.
Honor the journey of self-discovery; it leads to profound growth.	If you have money, you can make the ghosts and devils turn your grind stone.
Honor the past, live in the present, and dream of the future.	If you have never done anything evil, you should not be worrying about devils to know on your door.
Honor your intuition; it's the whisper of your inner wisdom.	If you judge people, you have no time to love them.
Honor your truth; it's the compass that guides you on your journey.	If you want happiness for a day, go fishing.
How can you expect to find ivory in a dog's mouth?	If you want happiness for a lifetime, help someone else.
How can you put out a fire set on a cart-load of firewood with only a cup of water?	If you want happiness for a month, get married.
How you look depends on where you go.	If you want happiness for a year, inherit a fortune.
Hug tightly those you love; their warmth brings comfort to the soul.	If you want happiness for an hour, take a nap.

44-3-45-67-35+17   18-68-20-60-12+11

56-49-27-58-60+8   42-19-12-50-16+13

37-46-18-48-12+16   39-59-33-31-56+19

38-59-41-57-33+3   37-9-43-44-7+1

30-36-49-65-63+25   48-26-28-60-18+8

69-30-7-29-64+4   34-31-35-63-7+23

40-19-29-16-26+25   29-39-26-64-40+13

62-15-53-10-14+21   40-67-50-37-38+6

56-54-40-6-21+9   17-32-46-58-47+9

14-43-6-45-5+25   39-4-25-30-3+16

6-27-39-34-55+23   16-7-29-63-11+13

18-45-62-60-37+6   5-69-1-33-46+19

61-25-27-64-54+18   19-55-29-5-31+19

If you want to get a sure crop with a big yield, sow wild oats.	Imagine the possibilities that lie ahead; your dreams hold infinite potential.
If you want to know how short a month is, ask someone who pays alimony.	Imagine the world as you wish to see it, then work to make it so.
If you wish good advice, consult your mother.	In order to take, one must first give.
If you're in a hurry you will never get there.	Infuse your actions with kindness; it creates ripple effects of positivity.
If your desires are not too extravagant they will be granted.	Inhale courage, exhale fear; bravery is the key to unlocking your potential.
Ignite the fire within you; passion fuels your journey to success.	Innovate with creativity; you have the ability to reshape your reality.
Ignite your imagination; it's the spark that ignites innovation.	Innovate with curiosity; the pursuit of knowledge opens doors to new horizons.
Ignite your passion for learning; knowledge is the key to personal growth.	Innovate with persistence; every setback is a stepping stone to success.
Illuminate the darkness with your inner light; positivity dispels negativity.	Innovate with resilience; adaptability is the cornerstone of progress.
Illuminate the world with your unique light; your presence is a gift.	Inspire greatness in yourself and others; belief is the seed of achievement.
Illuminate your path with positivity; optimism paves the way to greatness.	Inspire hope in others; your kindness has the power to uplift hearts.
Imagine the boundless possibilities of your future; the journey begins with a single step.	Inspire others with your actions; you have the power to make a difference.
Imagine the life you desire, then take bold steps to make it a reality.	Inspire others with your authenticity; your true self is your greatest gift.

51-1-47-52-20+21   61-29-66-51-44+13

56-58-68-8-4+21   44-33-12-37-48+14

64-14-40-11-24+10   66-69-30-61-2+9

15-6-60-40-46+19   3-40-2-48-10+15

36-7-61-18-65+16   67-49-20-21-10+11

30-49-25-8-62+16   39-47-9-24-19+13

12-29-18-44-56+16   10-69-13-36-22+12

34-28-1-22-56+9   41-19-31-69-35+25

68-23-53-20-23+4   38-65-47-2-65+24

32-26-59-22-29+5   19-53-12-48-11+13

5-17-16-26-43+16   14-63-24-57-55+15

68-41-59-34-14+18   69-49-35-58-37+15

21-14-31-25-37+4   61-13-4-56-34+23

Integrate love into every action; it's the universal language of the heart.	It is never too late to be what you might have been.
Integrate mindfulness into your daily life; presence brings clarity and peace.	It is often better not to see an insult than to avenge it.
Intuitively navigate life's twists and turns; your inner wisdom is your guide.	It is up to you to create your own adventures today!
Invest in meaningful connections; they enrich the fabric of your life.	It is very possible that you will achieve greatness in your lifetime.
Invest in your dreams with dedication; they are the seeds of your future.	It is wise reviewing old lessons.
Invest in yourself; self-care is the foundation of a fulfilling life.	It takes both sunshine and rain to make a rainbow.
Invite adventure into your life; it's where growth and discovery thrive.	It takes courage to admit fault.
Invite gratitude into your heart; it transforms ordinary moments into blessings.	It takes little effort to watch a man carry a load.
Invite joy into your life; it's the essence of true happiness.	It's time for you to explore all those new interests.
Invite serenity into your life; inner peace is the ultimate treasure.	Join hands with others in unity; together, we can accomplish great things.
It is easy to dodge a spear that comes in front of you but hard to keep harm away from an arrow shot from behind.	Jolt yourself out of complacency; greatness lies just beyond your comfort zone.
It is honorable to stand up for what is right, however unpopular it seems.	Journey inward to discover the vast universe within your soul.
It is most enjoyable to talk with you.	Journey towards your dreams with unwavering determination; success is on the horizon.

59-52-67-37-20+11   30-23-16-37-45+18

37-43-19-16-68+9   51-20-14-67-26+12

67-31-55-66-46+12   29-40-25-28-36+18

46-14-18-65-67+8   28-60-69-8-5+9

41-42-20-62-28+8   56-58-37-63-49+2

8-37-55-30-42+7   15-11-57-25-62+5

69-37-50-36-25+6   53-55-42-68-2+16

53-67-61-37-68+21   60-68-47-8-9+23

34-12-58-50-10+9   1-59-60-42-27+10

36-60-2-30-45+20   48-50-28-37-24+14

40-19-60-64-38+7   7-25-40-54-55+3

62-2-11-41-25+23   26-16-25-1-59+18

31-45-27-21-50+3   52-55-45-47-5+6

Journey with an open heart; it's the compass that guides you to your true north.	Joyfully embrace the diversity of life; it enriches the tapestry of humanity.
Journey with courage; the path to your dreams awaits your brave steps.	Joyfully embrace the journey of self-discovery; it leads to profound growth.
Journey with curiosity; each step forward brings new discoveries.	Joyfully embrace the present moment; it's where life's magic unfolds.
Journey with kindness in your heart; it creates ripples of compassion in the world.	Judge not the horse by his saddle.
Journey with purpose; let your passions be the fuel that propels you forward.	Juggle responsibilities with grace; you are capable of managing all that comes your way.
Journey with resilience; every setback is a lesson in disguise.	Jump at opportunities that come your way; they are stepping stones to your dreams.
Journeys are made richer with companionship; cherish those who walk beside you.	Jump fearlessly into the unknown; adventure awaits beyond your comfort zone.
Journeys are not always linear; embrace the detours, for they often lead to unexpected beauty.	Jumpstart your day with gratitude; it sets the tone for positivity.
Joy is contagious; spread it generously wherever you go.	Just as the river flows steadily towards the sea, so too does your path lead you to your destiny.
Joy is found in the connections we make with others; cherish each relationship as a gift.	Just as the stars illuminate the night sky, so too does your light shine bright in the world.
Joy is found in the simplest moments; cherish them as precious treasures.	Just as the sun rises each day, so too will new opportunities dawn for you.
Joy resides in the journey, not just the destination; savor each step along the way.	Just when you feel lost, remember that the stars guide you home.
Joy will come with the return of a good friend.	Just when you least expect it, a door of opportunity swings wide open before you.

55-13-63-57-25+4   50-42-68-69-26+11

4-27-45-28-46+23   69-56-57-28-68+2

56-18-22-44-69+10   15-40-44-6-14+6

33-2-13-69-61+10   49-29-28-67-16+4

57-12-19-40-47+11   4-12-33-11-54+3

66-54-62-25-12+7   56-26-42-39-53+11

4-38-66-16-40+15   59-25-13-65-44+16

67-69-47-15-55+5   26-2-34-50-47+10

37-10-27-38-53+2   53-35-4-42-35+10

35-25-58-44-37+1   25-40-7-64-49+25

57-24-2-52-9+24   51-13-41-1-29+23

51-6-9-66-17+14   18-50-42-29-27+24

7-28-68-35-2+25   66-28-65-50-63+6

Just when you think you've reached your limit, you discover new reservoirs of strength within.	Keep your focus on the present moment; it's where life's magic unfolds.
Juxtapose moments of stillness with bursts of creativity; balance is the key to harmony.	Keep your heart open to love; it's the most powerful force in the universe.
Keep a green tree in your heart and perhaps a singing bird will come.	Keep your intentions pure; they shape the energy you attract into your life.
Keep faith in the universe; it conspires in your favor more often than you realize.	Keep your mind open to new ideas; they may lead you to unexpected places.
Keep faith in yourself; you are capable of achieving your wildest dreams.	Keep your mind open to the beauty around you; it's everywhere, waiting to be discovered.
Keep laughter close at hand; it's the best medicine for the soul.	Keep your spirit adventurous; life's greatest treasures await the bold.
Keep moving forward, even in the face of adversity; resilience is your greatest strength.	Keep your spirit resilient; it's the armor that shields you from life's storms.
Keep striving for greatness; your potential knows no bounds.	Keep your spirit young at heart; it's the secret to a joyful life.
Keep true to the dreams of your youth.	Kind gestures have the power to brighten someone's day; spread them generously.
Keep your courage close at hand; it's the key to unlocking doors of opportunity.	Kind words have the power to heal wounds and mend hearts; use them often.
Keep your dreams alive; they are the seeds of your future success.	Kindness costs nothing but means everything; sprinkle it like confetti.
Keep your dreams close to your heart; they are the roadmap to your destiny.	Kindness is a bridge that connects souls; build it with care.
Keep your eyes on the stars, but remember to enjoy the journey along the way.	Kindness is a gift that keeps on giving; be generous with it always.

15-30-67-26-45+25   3-2-10-20-56+17

21-36-7-37-46+10   29-35-50-30-32+12

55-53-56-61-16+5   50-47-15-41-30+22

56-20-48-64-26+7   43-69-65-54-14+25

21-43-36-58-69+14   69-50-36-47-61+14

10-56-20-46-57+24   23-17-16-37-38+12

61-15-27-68-15+12   6-24-21-51-63+20

57-33-9-14-48+13   33-67-37-32-40+8

66-12-18-13-3+8   57-28-2-16-30+15

35-16-63-6-12+4   41-5-14-6-38+17

43-69-21-40-39+1   17-13-10-19-18+15

56-9-50-61-14+19   60-51-52-42-56+13

42-6-68-10-55+18   45-24-37-8-66+10

Kindness is a language that transcends barriers; speak it fluently.	Leap into each day with enthusiasm; it's the first step towards success.
Kindness is a ripple; watch as it spreads far and wide.	Leap over obstacles with grace; they are mere stepping stones on your journey.
Kindness is the currency of the heart; spend it lavishly and watch it multiply.	Learn from every experience; they are lessons in disguise.
Kindred souls find each other amidst life's chaos; treasure these connections.	Learn from the past, live in the present, and look forward to the future.
Kindred spirits are drawn together by invisible threads; cherish these connections.	Learning is a treasure that will follow its owner everywhere.
Know that within you lies the power to overcome any obstacle.	Let go of fear; it only holds you back from realizing your full potential.
Knowledge is a lifelong journey; embrace the lessons it brings.	Let go of judgment; acceptance opens the door to understanding.
Knowledge is the key that unlocks the doors of opportunity; pursue it eagerly.	Let go of what no longer serves you; it clears the path for new blessings.
Laugh at life's absurdities; humor is a powerful antidote to hardship.	Let gratitude be your daily companion; it opens doors to abundance.
Laugh often, for it is the music of the soul.	Let kindness be your default mode; it's a language understood by all.
Laws control the lesser man. Right conduct controls the greater one.	Let the world be filled with tranquility and goodwill.
Lean into life's challenges; they are opportunities for growth and resilience.	Let your dreams take flight; they are the wings that carry you to new heights.
Lean on others when you need support; community is a source of strength.	Let your intuition be your guide; it knows the way even when the path is unclear.

18-4-21-53-33+12	48-5-63-30-53+15
37-18-11-5-66+10	19-18-25-64-48+23
48-29-59-16-49+21	37-46-15-59-8+17
16-1-60-31-36+5	57-45-65-63-32+3
3-8-61-41-42+16	49-7-28-25-44+9
1-39-19-5-55+20	69-14-26-20-8+6
58-7-16-27-58+25	68-19-69-51-14+5
3-68-43-23-53+13	61-21-18-40-24+8
56-22-18-20-21+24	54-30-1-47-21+8
56-10-52-43-17+1	12-45-36-40-39+4
69-43-40-44-38+16	43-54-36-39-61+9
45-54-69-47-43+6	41-43-21-44-38+4
14-54-53-40-39+9	31-30-66-14-48+9

Let your light shine bright; the world needs your unique radiance.	Look! Good fortune is around you.
Let your passion be your fuel; it propels you towards your dreams.	Love deeply, for it is the greatest gift you can give and receive.
Life's greatest adventures begin with a single step; dare to take it.	Love is the answer to life's greatest questions; let it guide your actions.
Life's reward will be yours.	Love truth but pardon error.
Listen closely to the whispers of your heart; they lead you towards your true desires.	Love unconditionally; it has the power to transform hearts and minds.
Listen to the whispers of nature; they carry messages of wisdom and peace.	Love your neighbor, but do not pull down the fence.
Listen to the wisdom of elders; their experiences are priceless treasures.	Love yourself unconditionally; you are deserving of your own affection.
Listen to the wisdom of the old.	Magnify the beauty in the world; it's all around you, waiting to be seen.
Live authentically; there is power in embracing your true self.	Magnify your strengths and embrace your weaknesses; they make you unique.
Live boldly and fearlessly; the world is yours to explore.	Make connections that matter; they enrich the fabric of your life.
Live each day as if it were your masterpiece; you are the artist of your life.	Make each day count; life is a precious gift.
Look for beauty in unexpected places; it's all around you, waiting to be discovered.	Make gratitude your daily ritual; it opens the door to abundance.
Look for the silver lining in every cloud; optimism is a choice.	Make kindness your default mode; it has the power to transform lives.

12-30-34-16-69+18   66-20-34-39-59+17

27-14-43-47-11+6   38-1-61-64-68+2

32-20-36-19-43+19   67-45-44-69-38+15

35-57-69-13-37+3   49-24-35-10-8+20

63-15-18-14-25+6   56-21-64-35-27+14

68-63-34-69-53+22   41-58-19-13-69+21

14-57-25-19-24+18   14-20-3-27-62+12

30-56-14-40-16+5   9-33-62-20-44+11

69-51-2-50-62+4   3-45-36-64-17+10

34-61-5-35-31+16   38-26-58-44-46+4

56-3-65-49-43+14   58-53-57-55-5+10

23-34-42-47-1+20   35-3-66-10-42+13

46-69-8-22-4+2   18-25-29-2-16+1

Make peace with the past; it paves the way for a brighter future.	Manifest your dreams with unwavering belief; they are within your reach.
Make peace with uncertainty; it's the gateway to possibility.	Many new friends will be attracted to your friendly and charming ways.
Make room for growth in your life; change is the only constant.	Many people will be drawn to you for your wisdom and insights.
Make room for silence in your busy life; it's where clarity is found.	Many pleasurable and memorable adventures are in store for you!
Make space for joy in your life; it's the elixir of happiness.	Master the art of listening; it's a gift that deepens connections.
Make time for adventure; it keeps the spirit alive and curious.	Master the art of resilience; it's the key to overcoming any obstacle.
Make time for laughter; it's the sweetest melody for the soul.	Maximize each opportunity that comes your way; they are stepping stones to success.
Make time for self-care; it nourishes the soul and renews the spirit.	Maximize your potential; greatness lies within you.
Make your actions align with your values; integrity is your compass.	May you have great luck!
Make your dreams bigger than your fears; courage will carry you forward.	Meditation with an old enemy is advised.
Make your mark in whatever way you want.	Mend broken relationships with forgiveness and compassion.
Make your mark on the world; your legacy is waiting to be written.	Mend the pieces of your heart with love; it's the greatest healer.
Man's schemes are inferior to those made by heaven.	Mindfulness is the gateway to inner peace; cultivate it daily.

32-69-20-10-42+23   12-38-49-36-48+21

15-1-16-67-69+2   19-17-22-67-54+24

8-39-16-52-55+16   33-34-17-21-24+10

38-63-39-64-14+13   47-38-6-19-63+16

18-47-13-30-3+4   47-50-26-60-54+25

46-13-67-64-19+8   32-63-34-6-64+15

53-48-21-24-39+6   62-46-13-45-7+24

69-48-11-57-50+5   60-36-58-31-1+1

66-37-13-20-15+4   66-23-6-52-6+7

21-42-32-66-34+10   32-44-42-16-67+20

20-39-48-69-19+5   39-33-35-64-29+8

61-21-14-38-36+22   69-18-22-37-17+24

68-20-31-23-56+4   52-29-48-23-56+1

Mindset is everything; cultivate positivity and watch your world transform.	Never forget the power of love; it has the ability to heal and transform.
Miracles happen when you least expect them; keep your heart open.	Never give up on yourself; you are capable of achieving great things.
Money speaks a language everyone understands.	Never let fear dictate your decisions; courage leads to infinite possibilities.
Move forward with confidence; the universe conspires in your favor.	Never lose sight of your worth; you are deserving of love and respect.
Move forward with purpose; your destiny awaits your arrival.	Never stop at the weigh station on the road of life.
Move mountains with your determination; you are unstoppable.	Never underestimate the impact of a kind word or gesture; it can brighten someone's day.
Nature, time and patience are the three great physicians.	Never underestimate the power of kindness; it has the ability to change the world.
Navigate life's challenges with grace and resilience; you are stronger than you know.	New ideas could be profitable.
Navigate life's storms with courage and resilience; the sun always shines after the rain.	No challenge is too big for you.
Navigate life's twists and turns with patience and perseverance.	No harm in putting all your eggs in one basket - just watch it closely.
Navigate the journey of self-discovery with curiosity and openness.	No need to worry! You will always have everything that you need.
Navigate uncertainty with faith and trust in the journey ahead.	No one knows what he can do until he tries.
Never forget a friend, especially if he owes you.	No one remembers when you're right, but everyone remembers when you are wrong.

27-25-9-40-67+4   37-23-67-2-66+1

54-57-67-48-64+19   12-21-11-22-43+4

6-31-14-52-69+7   32-15-28-56-46+20

65-21-66-59-23+25   39-33-68-44-1+20

32-63-6-24-59+5   2-60-49-38-69+10

68-21-53-58-68+3   28-20-60-36-62+24

56-16-62-26-7+17   19-63-10-51-52+7

69-29-26-5-8+25   69-60-62-24-11+22

65-25-66-48-43+7   56-51-24-65-17+5

32-61-30-45-55+4   9-34-44-3-36+5

13-34-8-15-14+8   5-55-2-57-8+19

58-12-48-40-60+4   58-34-2-5-42+12

36-12-3-22-55+14   26-52-62-28-64+18

Not every soul can bear all things. Be practical.	Nurture the bonds of friendship with laughter and shared experiences.
Nothing gets in the way of your vision, except that very large brick wall locking your view.	Nurture the childlike wonder within you; it keeps life's adventures exciting.
Nothing in the world is accomplished without passion.	Nurture the light within you; it has the power to illuminate even the darkest of paths.
Notice the beauty in the ordinary; life's magic lies in the smallest of details.	Nurture your body with rest and nourishment; it's the vessel for your soul's journey.
Notice the blessings that surround you; gratitude opens doors to abundance.	Nurture your creativity; it's the wellspring of inspiration within you.
Notice the opportunities that present themselves; seize them with enthusiasm.	Nurture your dreams with action; they are the blueprints for your future.
Notice the signs and synchronicities that guide you along your path.	Nurture your dreams with care; they are the seeds of your future.
Nourish your soul with moments of stillness and reflection; inner peace awaits.	Nurture your heart with forgiveness; it sets you free from the burdens of the past.
Now is a good time to buy stock.	Nurture your mind with knowledge; it's the key to unlocking new possibilities.
Now is the best time to try something new.	Nurture your passions and watch them grow into something beautiful.
Now it is best to take things just one step at a time.	Nurture your relationships like precious flowers; they bloom with love and care.
Nurture a sense of wonder for the world around you; it keeps life's mysteries alive.	Nurture your spirit with love and compassion; it's the fuel for your inner fire.
Nurture a spirit of adventure; life's greatest treasures await the bold.	Observe the beauty in imperfection; it adds depth to life's canvas.

40-44-49-69-1+3

31-53-55-33-54+16

23-18-35-48-1+11

53-9-46-4-6+13

6-4-16-26-36+24

49-20-29-30-46+13

69-13-60-22-48+18

11-20-69-12-8+14

2-51-21-56-7+19

65-9-31-54-60+16

1-19-10-53-26+25

65-50-1,57-7-43+6

10-60-53-48-65+10

55-46-41-42-19+23

31-24-8-28-47+18

56-18-24-58-14+9

8-23-5-45-39+4

14-50-53-5-33+2

64-10-22-66-7+5

20-48-38-44-60+11

22-53-49-10-19+4

44-33-66-42-38+16

12-36-34-46-39+8

60-22-47-12-23+5

67-42-25-26-40+10

40-26-64-53-35+2

Observe the beauty in nature; it's a reminder of life's wonders.	Open your eyes to the miracles around you; they are everywhere, waiting to be seen.
Observe the patterns of life; they reveal the interconnectedness of all things.	Open your heart to forgiveness; it's the key to inner peace.
Observe the rhythm of life; it's a dance of endless possibilities.	Open your heart to new possibilities; they are the seeds of transformation.
Observe the symphony of life; each note plays a part in the grand composition.	Open your mind to different perspectives; they expand your understanding of the world.
Offer compassion to yourself and others; it's the language of the heart.	Open your mind to endless possibilities; the universe is abundant with opportunities.
Offer encouragement to those in need; your words have the power to uplift.	Open your soul to love; it's the most powerful force in the universe.
Offer kindness freely; it's a gift that costs nothing but means everything.	Opportunities are like sunrises; if you wait too long, you might miss them.
Offer your talents to the world; they are your unique gifts to share.	Opportunity knocks softly; listen closely and be ready to answer.
One cannot know the best that is in him.	Opt for gratitude in every circumstance; it transforms challenges into blessings.
One must know that there is a path at the end of the road.	Opt for optimism; it brightens even the darkest of days.
One who admires you greatly is hidden before your eyes.	Opt for simplicity in a complex world; it brings clarity and peace.
Only you can decide what is important to you.	Optimize each moment; life is too short for regrets.
Open your arms to embrace change; it brings growth and new beginnings.	Optimize your potential; you are capable of achieving greatness.

24-69-69-53-13+22   37-62-25-13-65+14

55-34-7-69-41+10   5-49-47-18-49+18

6-67-62-34-36+25   17-31-61-69-5+10

6-4-63-9-36+11   26-57-37-45-17+15

56-39-33-45-61+25   28-11-21-56-55+22

57-40-31-20-19+25   7-27-45-54-50+23

3-32-25-35-7+13   17-69-47-38-62+11

19-53-61-23-63+4   7-53-58-6-45+21

14-61-69-60-12+21   30-36-2-18-30+1

69-12-15-1-65+8   46-18-52-24-27+3

43-40-62-50-8+7   36-59-13-6-67+23

33-53-18-37-38+12   27-13-15-7-44+4

18-55-6-33-29+2   57-16-11-63-9+3

Others can help you now.	Passionate new romance appears in your life when you least expect it.
Others respect you deeply.	Patience is a virtue; trust in divine timing.
Overcome fear with courage; it's the gateway to growth.	Patience is the best remedy for every trouble.
Overcome obstacles with resilience; they are stepping stones to your success.	Patience is the key to joy.
Own your choices; they shape the path you walk.	Pave your own path in life; your journey is unique and beautiful.
Own your journey; your path is uniquely yours to walk.	Pay attention to the whispers of intuition; they are your inner compass.
Own your power; it resides within you, waiting to be unleashed.	Pennies from heaven find their way to your doorstep this year!
Own your story; it's what makes you beautifully unique.	Perceive challenges as opportunities for growth; they shape your character.
Own your worth; you are deserving of love and respect.	Perseverance is the key to success; keep moving forward with determination.
Pack your bags. You're bound for an exciting destination.	Persevere in the face of adversity; your strength lies in resilience.
Paint your future with hope; it colors the canvas of your destiny.	Pick the flower when it's ready to be picked.
Paint your world with vibrant colors; life is your masterpiece.	Place special emphasis on old friendship.
Pardon is the choicest flower of victory.	Plan for many pleasures ahead.

23-17-16-63-60+12   40-10-55-20-69+3

4-39-23-15-26+8   4-19-19-21-17+25

8-53-32-22-34+23   67-47-24-34-22+24

6-49-43-26-9+23   37-66-1-68-62+20

60-37-47-66-58+24   46-67-17-59-48+17

66-5-50-69-60+22   5-57-36-63-46+12

4-58-46-2-26+20   24-21-53-13-10+21

69-20-22-8-37+15   25-5-28-38-52+21

54-64-11-12-67+9   29-31-11-24-69+23

46-7-35-6-15+1   6-51-67-44-10+11

56-16-63-4-28+12   38-14-38-3-56+14

33-69-2-8-14+10   69-47-61-3-28+11

54-58-47-50-43+11   63-15-61-35-38+22

Plant seeds of kindness wherever you go; they blossom into beautiful connections.	Promise only what you can deliver.
Plant seeds of positivity in your thoughts and watch them bloom into reality.	Promises are like babies; fun to make but hard to deliver.
Plant seeds of wisdom in your actions; they bear fruit in the garden of life.	Promote love and acceptance; they are the foundations of a harmonious world.
Playfully embrace life's adventures; laughter is the best medicine.	Promote peace wherever you go; it starts with the kindness in your heart.
Possibilities are endless; believe in the magic of what could be.	Propel yourself towards your dreams with passion and purpose.
Practice forgiveness; it frees your spirit and heals your heart.	Prosperity makes friends and adversity tries them.
Practice gratitude daily; it opens doors to abundance and joy.	Protect your dreams fiercely; they are the essence of your soul.
Practice mindfulness; savor the present moment and all its wonders.	Protect your energy; surround yourself with positivity and love.
Practice patience; great things take time to unfold.	Protective measures will prevent costly disasters.
Prejudice is the child of ignorance.	Pursue adventures that ignite your soul; life is meant to be lived fully.
Press on with courage; every step forward is a victory.	Pursue authenticity in all that you do; your true self is your greatest asset.
Prioritize inner peace; it's the foundation of a balanced life.	Pursue your passions with relentless determination; they are the fuel for your dreams.
Prioritize self-care; nourish your mind, body, and soul.	Pursuit of knowledge is a lifelong journey; embrace learning with curiosity.

57-2-64-33-67+20

67-32-6-28-69+1

41-67-32-69-50+10

11-19-47-69-67+20

32-33-38-69-49+3

24-28-22-14-9+19

14-24-40-6-34+14

63-11-22-21-36+21

36-61-29-44-51+25

60-47-36-25-7+23

64-15-54-66-48+17

29-20-53-41-32+25

49-2-22-32-45+16

53-53-60-28-26+20

39-62-53-10-23+16

63-50-42-46-9+24

57-4-14-57-45+25

44-27-40-46-15+25

34-33-53-59-31+12

56-59-49-55-45+1

21-52-59-58-42+17

43-68-32-3-19+6

34-45-62-6-8+21

32-26-45-3-22+25

66-6-32-18-63+18

27-7-44-26-12+2

Push beyond your comfort zone; growth happens when you challenge yourself.

Qualify your friendships with sincerity and loyalty; they are treasures to be cherished.

Qualify your goals with specificity; clarity breeds accomplishment.

Quash negativity with positivity; it's the antidote to life's challenges.

Quell the storm within with the calm of your spirit; peace is found within.

Quell your anxieties with the certainty of your inner strength.

Quell your doubts with faith in your abilities; you are capable of greatness.

Quell your fears with courage; they are but shadows in the light of your strength.

Quench your soul's longing for connection with acts of kindness and compassion.

Quench your thirst for adventure; life's greatest treasures await the bold.

Quench your thirst for growth with a commitment to lifelong learning.

Quest for knowledge with insatiable curiosity; it opens doors to new worlds.

Question the status quo; innovation springs from the courage to challenge.

Question with boldness; seek truth with an open heart and mind.

Question with curiosity; answers lie in the depths of inquiry.

Question your assumptions; wisdom lies in seeking deeper understanding.

Quicken your heartbeat with the thrill of possibility; life is an exhilarating journey.

Quicken your pace towards self-discovery; the journey is an endless revelation.

Quicken your pace towards your dreams; the journey is yours to embark upon.

Quicken your pulse with the excitement of new beginnings.

Quicken your senses to the beauty that surrounds you; it's a feast for the soul.

Quicken your steps towards your aspirations; they are waiting to be realized.

Quiet your mind and listen to the whispers of your heart; it knows the way.

Quietly embrace solitude; it's where you reconnect with your true self.

Quietly honor the wisdom of your ancestors; their legacy lives on within you.

Quietly observe life's beauty; it's often found in the smallest of details.

20-54-46-34-44+8   53-55-60-61-8+11

21-28-46-30-13+8   36-61-3-27-58+9

37-27-5-68-49+24   8-13-5-64-22+24

40-26-33-44-26+11   69-31-68-42-9+4

10-6-47-14-16+12   17-36-46-68-31+20

22-20-4-20-10+3   53-27-54-8-18+16

40-60-14-66-14+11   46-55-65-48-30+18

24-9-66-25-3+5   46-11-50-58-57+6

6-65-22-36-66+13   69-24-67-11-6+8

56-34-4-64-30+4   22-29-45-56-64+16

20-47-41-67-52+5   45-54-69-17-51+14

64-54-31-7-34+15   23-12-15-58-23+21

63-16-60-13-40+7   22-24-47-35-23+9

Quietly reflect on the lessons of the past; they are stepping stones to the future.	Recognize the beauty in diversity; it enriches our world.
Quilt together the moments of your life into a tapestry of memories.	Reconcile with an old friend. All has been forgotten.
Quiver with anticipation for the adventures that lie ahead.	Reconnect with old friends; they bring warmth to your soul.
Quiver with excitement for the possibilities that await you.	Reflect on your blessings; gratitude opens doors to abundance.
Quota your time wisely; invest it in pursuits that nourish your soul.	Reframe setbacks as opportunities for growth; they are blessings in disguise.
Radiant smiles are windows to the soul; let yours shine brightly.	Rejoice in the journey of self-discovery; it leads to inner peace.
Radiate love and kindness; they are the purest forms of energy.	Relax and enjoy yourself.
Radiate positivity wherever you go; it's contagious and uplifting.	Release expectations and embrace the journey; it's where growth happens.
Rally your courage in times of doubt; you are braver than you think.	Release the past; the future holds endless possibilities.
Reach for the stars; your dreams are within your grasp.	Remain true to yourself; authenticity is your greatest strength.
Reach out to others in times of need; compassion heals.	Remember to be gentle with yourself; you are a work in progress.
Realize your potential; you are capable of achieving greatness.	Remember to breathe deeply and find peace in the moment.
Recharge your spirit in moments of solitude and reflection.	Remember to nourish your spirit with love and kindness.

9-34-11-55-38+21   31-22-50-15-24+16

22-47-45-54-1+23   55-24-20-63-34+8

21-57-16-43-63+6   59-22-66-49-3+5

17-18-5-23-32+25   52-51-53-31-24+20

35-68-35-9-18+20   55-67-23-49-19+20

57-39-67-21-26+9   33-45-3-43-31+19

16-3-37-32-12+20   32-52-21-39-47+1

58-47-15-41-48+23   33-63-30-40-25+7

3-24-62-50-60+18   26-57-31-18-65+20

48-34-55-16-12+10   61-17-25-16-30+23

21-5-18-55-25+2   7-4-46-45-69+23

23-43-62-67-16+6   61-60-12-2-11+3

40-55-13-16-62+21   39-56-35-42-9+3

Renew your commitment to self-improvement every day.	Rise to the challenge; greatness awaits those who dare.
Rest has a peaceful effect on your physical and emotional health.	Rise with the sun and seize the day; it's full of promise.
Rest is a good thing, but boredom is its brother.	Romance moves you in a new direction.
Resting well is as important as working hard.	Savor the simple pleasures of life; they bring the greatest joy.
Restrain yourself from intruding in others' business.	Savor your freedom -- it is precious.
Revel in the beauty of each moment; life is a precious gift.	Say hello to others. You will have a happier day.
Revel in the joy of simple pleasures; they bring richness to life.	See the beauty in every moment; it's all around you, waiting to be noticed.
Revel in the magic of nature; it reminds us of life's wonders.	Seek out opportunities for growth in every experience.
Rewrite your story with each new day; you hold the pen to your destiny.	Seek wisdom from the past; it illuminates the path forward.
Ride the waves of change with grace; they lead to new horizons.	Seize opportunities with confidence and conviction.
Ripples of kindness have the power to change the world.	Seize the day with courage and determination; it's yours to conquer.
Rise above challenges with resilience; they make you stronger.	Self-knowledge is a life long process.
Rise above negativity; focus on the positive and watch it multiply.	Set boundaries to protect your peace and well-being.

56-21-58-46-58+20   10-6-47-69-30+7

45-13-34-27-58+3   6-34-65-22-64+10

12-50-19-61-51+24   36-2-47-16-22+2

3-54-59-14-64+9   15-40-62-4-38+25

53-42-62-44-8+5   36-23-30-38-34+10

12-56-69-56-2+16   28-52-69-37-6+5

12-32-2-60-44+5   54-30-8-13-58+20

46-38-34-10-8+19   63-18-66-33-48+22

32-28-37-23-35+2   69-21-39-64-47+4

37-18-57-64-44+24   68-6-55-61-15+7

21-64-4-58-54+16   39-62-17-55-7+15

25-2-68-69-57+16   1-1-31-21-65+6

50-38-42-69-40+8   31-25-50-59-53+18

Set goals that inspire you; they are the roadmap to your dreams.	Someone will invite you to a party.
Share your heart with the world; vulnerability is a strength.	Someone will visit you soon.
Share your talents with the world; they are gifts meant to be shared.	Something nice is coming to you in the mail.
Shine brightly like a star; the world needs your light.	Sometimes a stranger can bring great meaning to your life.
Silence your inner critic and listen to your inner champion.	Sparkle with enthusiasm; your energy is contagious.
Small confidences mark the onset of a friendship.	Speak only well of people and you need never whisper.
Smile often; it's a language understood by all.	Spread joy wherever you go; it's the ripple effect of kindness.
Smile to others, honesty and friendship bring you fortune.	Spread kindness like sunshine; it brightens even the darkest of days.
Smile when you are ready.	Spread love like wildfire; it's the most powerful force in the universe.
Soar above limitations and reach for the stars.	Stand firm in your beliefs; they are the foundation of who you are.
Some people never have anything except ideas. Go do it.	Stand tall in the face of adversity; you are stronger than you know.
Some pursue happiness; you create it.	Stay close to your inner self, you will benefit in many ways.
Someone is speaking well of you.	Stay curious; there is always something new to learn.

66-1-36-37-35+22   41-7-6-4-5+9

66-36-51-23-9+6   15-67-54-39-55+13

17-14-63-52-56+7   1-14-16-34-9+12

69-10-48-17-26+5   10-14-65-53-54+4

25-64-1-47-57+13   69-39-8-14-56+18

8-66-53-62-69+10   3-14-5-47-8+16

8-54-25-64-35+13   55-33-56-60-57+3

15-20-67-1-10+20   26-69-61-20-64+24

40-45-42-31-57+15   53-4-61-13-15+25

38-7-4-31-38+14   51-55-22-32-26+15

20-47-67-31-46+12   20-46-66-1-12+17

28-12-6-39-38+12   17-67-22-5-58+21

37-62-67-50-22+10   11-33-13-24-5+25

Stay true to yourself; authenticity is your greatest strength.	Take advantage of your great imagination. It will serve you well.
Stop searching; happiness is just next to you.	Take delight in the simple pleasures of life; they bring lasting happiness.
Strengthen your spirit with gratitude; it's a powerful force for good.	Take initiative and create the life you desire; you hold the pen to your story.
Strive for balance in all areas of your life; it leads to harmony.	Take risks and embrace new adventures; they lead to growth and discovery.
Strive for excellence in all that you do; mediocrity has no place in greatness.	Take small steps towards your goals every day; progress adds up.
Strive for perfection but don't become too obsessed about it.	Take solace in the beauty of nature; it brings peace to the soul.
Strive for progress, not perfection; every step forward counts.	Take the high road.
Stupidity will get you into messes, but it will not get you out of them.	Take time to appreciate the present moment; it is where life truly happens.
Support others on their journey; we rise by lifting each other.	Take time to rest and recharge; self-care is essential for well-being.
Surround yourself with laughter; it's the soundtrack of a happy life.	Tap into your inner strength and face challenges with courage.
Surround yourself with love and positivity; it's the key to happiness.	That special someone may simply be waiting for you.
Surround yourself with supportive people who lift you higher.	The arrogant army will lose the battle for sure.
Take advantage of an opportunity to make money	The best times of your life have not yet been lived.

27-31-19-60-55+15		62-44-18-63-21+3

38-58-48-21-62+2		62-3-3-18-22+5

16-52-1-9-42+25		59-6-58-67-50+4

26-13-24-10-49+12		55-35-8-19-14+17

60-58-54-28-63+21		7-5-16-20-27+21

18-19-59-28-57+21		34-45-2-11-20+24

34-25-6-57-3+5		32-40-9-5-56+17

9-12-51-53-9+23		18-40-8-23-25+3

35-38-17-23-39+10		6-59-26-35-15+19

37-59-53-31-17+13		55-30-60-27-41+18

13-22-26-43-34+1		12-62-49-27-7+2

28-7-10-5-28+7		57-17-67-59-27+21

18-65-17-69-62+21		1-67-13-47-14+18

The care and sensitivity you show towards others will return to you.	The one who says it cannot be done should never interrupt the one who is doing it.
The courage to be great lies deep within each of us.	The pleasure of what we enjoy is lost by wanting more.
The daughter of a crab does not give birth to a bird.	The road less traveled is that way for a reason.
The entire world may not have a lover; but they will be watching him.	The secret of getting ahead is getting started.
The eyes believe themselves; the ears believe other people.	The secret of staying young is good health and lying about your age.
The face of nature reflects all of life's ups and downs.	The secret to good friends is no secret to you.
The faith you seek lives within you.	The small steps you take will ultimately bring you great fortune.
The fun side of a relationship begins to unfold.	The smart thing to do is to begin trusting your intuitions.
The greater part of inspiration is perspiration.	The soldier who retreated 50 paces jeered at the one who retreated 100 paces.
The hard times will begin to fade. Joy will take their place.	The stars appear every night in the sky. All is well.
The journey of a thousand miles starts with a single step.	The strong person understands how to withstand substantial loss.
The joyfulness of a man prolongs his days.	The superior person is modest in speech but exceeds in action.
The longer the night lasts, the more our dreams will be.	The things that come to those who wait may be the things left by those who got there first.

31-56-13-27-40+20   62-65-59-4-39+24

47-31-17-10-41+9   66-35-15-50-48+18

68-35-17-57-37+16   58-12-63-54-33+18

64-36-40-44-62+2   15-60-46-23-41+8

42-15-54-23-44+24   19-4-18-22-69+4

67-13-67-19-27+17   46-39-42-68-28+16

32-54-56-51-43+9   69-3-59-49-58+4

15-35-11-45-36+7   5-3-6-63-67+13

64-25-3-62-65+17   31-20-15-50-10+8

29-37-17-59-53+13   54-13-25-9-55+18

22-34-69-17-6+7   40-14-30-27-8+25

1-2-65-28-11+1   14-54-11-43-8+12

43-60-55-68-24+5   4-61-37-23-18+10

The time is right to make new friends.	There is no wave without wind.
The truly generous person shares, even with the undeserving.	There is no wisdom greater than kindness.
The wheel of good fortune is finally turning in your direction!	There is someone owing you many thanks.
There appear to be many clouds; but they quickly pass.	There will be many surprises; unexpected gains are likely.
There are days in a year, may all of your dreams come true.	There will be plenty of time to work hard; enjoy yourself!
There are many fish in the sea, throw this one back.	There will be someone sharing your warmth.
There are many new opportunities that are being presented to you.	Things in life should be simple rather than complex.
There are many unexpected & thrilling surprises in store for you!	This is a smooth long journey with great expectations.
There are no shortcuts to any place worth going.	This is really a lovely day. Congratulations!
There is a good chance of a romantic encounter soon.	This is the month when ingenuity stands high on the list.
There is beauty in simplicity.	This year will bring you great happiness.
There is no mistake as great as that of being right always.	Those that care will make the effort.
There is no rose without a thorn.	Those who never climb, never reach the top.

29-16-65-69-17+3   23-3-59-66-44+10

22-21-3-10-18+14   12-42-38-29-4+10

62-3-49-16-52+5   53-60-58-19-66+15

42-5-51-43-59+8   54-20-48-26-49+22

21-14-29-44-48+13   68-19-25-21-8+19

17-42-58-38-17+19   66-39-19-2-13+21

37-20-44-26-7+3   42-28-50-24-34+6

65-66-16-28-22+10   20-63-50-32-58+5

42-51-12-32-27+24   64-62-49-31-19+1

58-4-11-15-69+23   35-41-9-44-41+2

62-19-10-42-66+3   3-23-41-52-55+17

56-20-56-4-69+15   26-55-18-7-65+25

51-64-44-13-3+3   43-65-5-48-68+1

Through greater effort and hard work, a precious dream comes true.	Transform setbacks into stepping stones towards success.
Tiger father begets tiger son.	Traveling more often is important for your health and happiness.
Time and patience are called for, many surprises await you!	Traveling this year will bring your life into greater perspective.
Time is precious, but truth is more precious than time.	Treasure each moment with loved ones; they are precious and fleeting.
Time is the wisest counselor.	Treasure the diversity of perspectives and experiences in the world.
To know is to know nothing. That is the true meaning of knowledge.	Treasure the journey as much as the destination; each step has its own magic.
To love and win is the best thing; to love and lose the next best.	Treasure the lessons learned from both success and failure.
Today is your lucky day.	Treasure the moments of joy and find beauty in the ordinary.
Transform challenges into opportunities for growth and resilience.	Treasure the relationships that bring love and support into your life.
Transform challenges into opportunities for learning and growth.	Treasure the wisdom of the past; it guides you on your journey.
Transform dreams into reality with determination and perseverance.	Treasure what you have.
Transform fear into courage and uncertainty into faith.	Treasure your good memories and you need not worry about ending a banquet.
Transform negative thoughts into positive affirmations; belief shapes reality.	Triumph over adversity with resilience and determination.

36-33-37-54-68+20   65-15-33-4-56+22

24-3-36-20-21+9   39-2-27-55-7+5

65-12-3-14-9+25   55-33-24-32-18+10

25-9-6-24-33+21   41-6-63-5-13+4

66-60-31-58-7+11   40-33-38-50-35+3

3-61-11-10-40+24   69-20-40-34-59+25

53-19-55-10-41+12   6-13-44-64-37+11

9-29-42-58-27+12   47-54-49-3-68+12

63-27-63-69-20+6   64-41-3-35-11+4

30-52-65-46-31+8   45-30-36-17-29+4

8-14-57-4-53+20   67-56-49-64-34+11

14-52-34-62-10+22   31-57-18-37-42+4

10-55-62-45-61+13   15-58-21-10-46+17

Trust in the journey, even when the path is uncertain.	Unburden yourself from the weight of the past; forgiveness sets you free.
Trust in the power of kindness; it has the ability to change lives.	Uncover the beauty in everyday moments; they are the building blocks of joy.
Trust in the process of life; it has a way of working out in the end.	Uncover your passions and pursue them with unwavering dedication.
Trust in the timing of the universe; everything unfolds as it should.	Understand that challenges are opportunities in disguise; they propel you forward.
Trust in your inner wisdom and let it guide you forward.	Understand that every ending is a new beginning in disguise.
Trust in yourself and your abilities; you are capable of great things.	Understand that growth often comes from discomfort; embrace the journey.
Trust your intuition. The universe is guiding your life.	Unearth the treasures within your heart; they are the keys to fulfillment.
Try a new system or different approach.	Unexpected romantic and financial gifts surprise and delight you!
Try not to stand on your own side during an argument.	Unify your goals with a clear vision and purpose; they guide your journey.
Try something new and different you will like the results.	Unify your mind, body, and spirit; harmony brings balance and peace.
Try something new, you might be pleasantly surprised.	Unite with others in compassion and understanding; together, we are stronger.
Tune into the rhythm of nature; it restores balance and harmony.	Unite your dreams with action; determination paves the way to success.
Tune into your intuition; it is a powerful guide on your journey.	Unleash your creativity and let your imagination soar to new heights.

19-11-55-64-19+14   24-69-28-58-57+11

51-53-9-36-50+12   47-44-37-54-16+13

56-64-34-16-38+22   56-47-54-59-48+2

63-38-26-10-23+18   51-10-43-53-26+13

17-23-21-40-23+22   47-67-47-10-65+17

38-48-69-11-69+9   25-24-59-54-6+1

59-61-4-32-18+24   28-60-61-46-52+12

69-48-52-62-6+7   7-30-66-59-52+11

60-10-12-1-31+3   48-47-69-13-12+18

38-48-58-33-69+21   43-41-47-19-43+17

47-6-14-29-8+2   42-17-29-69-10+7

6-3-36-36-31+7   68-17-45-32-46+16

66-41-65-50-8+17   69-57-9-52-62+6

Unleash your potential and embrace the boundless possibilities of the universe.	Uplift others with words of encouragement and acts of kindness.
Unlock the doors of perception and see the world with fresh eyes.	Uplift your spirits with laughter and joy; they are the elixirs of life.
Unravel the complexities of life with curiosity and wonder.	Use your eloquence where it will do the most good.
Unravel the mysteries of your soul through self-reflection and introspection.	Utilize each day as an opportunity to learn, grow, and evolve.
Unveil the beauty of diversity and celebrate the richness it brings.	Utilize setbacks as stepping stones to greater resilience and wisdom.
Unveil your true self to the world; authenticity is your greatest gift.	Utilize your talents and abilities to make a positive impact in the world.
Unwind and find solace in moments of stillness and tranquility.	Validate your dreams with action; they are the blueprints of your destiny.
Unwind the layers of fear and doubt; beneath lies your true potential.	Validate your emotions with compassion; they are a guiding compass.
Uphold courage in the face of uncertainty; it is the catalyst for growth.	Validate your unique gifts and talents; they are your contribution to the world.
Uphold gratitude as a daily practice; it transforms perspective and mindset.	Validate your worthiness; you are deserving of love and respect.
Uphold kindness as your guiding principle; it fosters connection and empathy.	Value the friendships that enrich your life; they are priceless treasures.
Uphold the power of love as a force for healing and transformation.	Value the lessons learned from both success and failure; they shape your journey.
Uphold your values with integrity; they are the pillars of your character.	Value the moments of stillness and silence; they reveal profound truths.

26-67-64-57-39+24   26-44-17-48-2+5

53-39-17-18-45+8   42-15-12-40-30+17

21-28-69-23-42+3   44-10-38-48-30+15

35-31-6-29-23+9   9-40-67-15-4+25

9-57-24-67-56+9   3-28-59-8-55+25

47-12-16-35-9+13   49-44-32-29-25+16

60-13-25-64-49+16   12-34-21-53-46+4

18-69-48-34-42+3   5-44-69-63-56+4

6-4-57-4-22+10   15-7-67-69-65+11

28-1-25-5-40+18   43-52-31-36-57+12

64-57-32-18-1+12   66-22-48-63-38+14

19-42-9-22-69+19   25-18-43-2-51+24

50-16-10-14-63+17   28-47-54-68-14+2

Vanish negativity with positivity; optimism is a powerful force.	View setbacks as detours, not dead ends; resilience leads you forward.
Vanquish self-doubt with confidence; you are more capable than you realize.	Visualize a world filled with peace, love, and understanding; it begins with you.
Venture boldly towards your goals; the universe conspires in your favor.	Visualize success with unwavering belief; your mindset shapes your reality.
Venture forth with curiosity and wonder; life is an endless exploration.	Visualize your dreams with clarity and conviction; they are within your reach.
Venture into nature's embrace; it restores balance and harmony.	Vitalize your body, mind, and soul with nourishing practices.
Venture into the future with hope and optimism; the best is yet to come.	Vitalize your relationships with communication and connection.
Venture into the unknown with courage; therein lies the magic of discovery.	Vitalize your spirit with acts of kindness and compassion.
Venture outside your comfort zone; growth thrives in the realm of discomfort.	Voice your appreciation for the beauty that surrounds you; it amplifies joy.
Very often you cannot help thinking of somebody.	Voice your gratitude for the blessings in your life; it multiplies abundance.
Vibrate with positivity; your energy attracts abundance and joy.	Voice your truth with authenticity; it resonates with the power of authenticity.
Vicious as a tigress can be, she never eats her own cubs.	Vow to live each day with purpose and intention; it's the key to fulfillment.
View challenges as opportunities for growth and transformation.	Voyage through life with an open heart and open mind.
View challenges as opportunities to showcase your strength and resilience.	Waiting for a rabbit to hit upon a tree and be killed in order to catch it.

44-29-57-40-68+11   6-63-15-41-24+9

23-1-3-24-55+25   49-64-69-32-65+20

52-20-45-17-46+21   48-15-51-25-68+22

11-61-14-52-49+11   13-21-7-58-8+17

49-12-18-16-25+7   55-5-2-15-57+2

69-52-57-4-24+18   43-9-51-9-46+7

35-66-69-43-39+18   68-35-59-41-33+4

13-41-30-66-5+1   24-49-55-14-69+7

20-63-64-69-18+25   2-14-13-42-67+17

20-26-6-10-58+2   17-34-20-56-7+15

23-25-51-48-39+16   65-49-13-15-41+19

34-48-11-54-37+21   4-50-2-7-39+10

11-13-33-47-16+19   8-32-21-11-37+4

Wake up each day with gratitude in your heart; it sets the tone for a beautiful day.	Weather life's storms with resilience and grace; they pave the way for brighter days.
Walk in the footsteps of those who inspire you; their wisdom lights your path.	Weave together the threads of love and understanding in all your relationships.
Walk with integrity and honor; your character is your most valuable asset.	Welcome new beginnings with open arms; they bring fresh opportunities for growth.
Walk your own path with confidence and conviction; it leads to true fulfillment.	Welcome setbacks as opportunities for growth; they refine you like gold in the fire.
Wander down paths of curiosity and exploration; you never know what treasures you may find.	Welcome the unknown with a spirit of curiosity and excitement; it holds infinite possibilities.
Wander off the beaten path and discover hidden gems that await your exploration.	What has hidden itself in the shadows will become clear to you.
Wanderlust is a beautiful thing; let your adventurous spirit guide you to new horizons.	What makes an apple fall to the ground?
Warm your heart with acts of kindness; they create a ripple effect of positivity.	What you left behind is more mellow than wine.
Watch as challenges transform into stepping stones towards your dreams.	When anger arises, think of the consequences.
Watch as the seeds of kindness you sow blossom into beautiful connections.	When both feet are planted firmly, nothing can shake you.
Watch for signs and synchronicities that guide you on your journey; trust in their wisdom.	When the ear will not listen to the fool, the heart escapes sorrow.
Watch your relations with other people carefully, be reserved.	When the ear will not listen to the wise ones, the heart may experience sorrow.
We are not so much concerned if you are slow as when you come to a halt.	If you are poor, neighbors won't visit; If rich, you'll receive visits from alleged relatives afar.

59-15-13-18-28+25

43-11-15-57-44+23

29-43-38-66-5+15

50-13-52-44-65+5

56-59-39-36-41+19

34-15-27-46-7+10

22-20-15-63-55+23

37-41-22-17-59+19

48-24-56-49-8+6

47-54-9-4-69+14

14-49-33-47-57+2

13-36-43-25-21+21

21-57-25-4-28+13

3-15-39-60-5+7

57-56-34-26-20+20

41-20-69-33-22+12

18-33-16-28-59+12

41-6-19-56-18+13

33-59-14-54-60+11

60-26-48-66-28+18

48-11-7-8-15+18

38-69-33-56-20+18

26-11-65-10-56+19

1-25-69-9-24+17

23-53-13-11-6+21

60-40-8-67-21+2

When you expect your opponent to yield, you also should avoid hurting him.	Witness the beauty in diversity; it enriches the tapestry of human experience.
When you have musk, you will automatically have fragrance.	Witness the beauty of nature's miracles; they remind us of the wonder of life.
When you learn to be flexible, amazing opportunities reveal themselves!	Wonderful is a beautiful word.
Whisper words of encouragement to yourself; you are your own greatest cheerleader.	Words are the voice of the heart.
Whisper your dreams to the universe and trust that they will be heard.	Work diligently towards your goals; each step forward brings you closer to success.
Win or lose, always learn from every experience; they are stepping stones to wisdom.	Work towards inner peace and harmony; it is the foundation of a meaningful life.
Wisdom is the principal thing.	Working with children has a miraculous effect on your spirits.
Wish for the courage to follow your heart's true desires; it knows the way to your true purpose.	Wrestle with challenges knowing that each obstacle you overcome makes you stronger.
Wish for the happiness and fulfillment of others; your generosity of spirit will be rewarded.	Wrestle with doubt and fear, but never let them hold you back from greatness.
Wish for the strength to overcome adversity; resilience is your greatest ally.	Wrestle with uncertainty knowing that every challenge you face is a chance to grow.
Wish upon stars and believe in the magic of your dreams; they hold the power to manifest.	X marks the spot where your dreams await; set sail and discover them.
With a few changes, change will be made.	Xamine your beliefs and be open to new perspectives.
With a little more hard work, your creativity takes you to great heights!	Xamine your fears and confront them with courage and compassion.

6-3-31-43-24+10   12-55-18-58-63+13

6-20-1-43-68+11   52-8-33-63-43+25

30-26-58-4-28+7   11-51-21-66-31+1

30-43-53-12-13+3   49-19-4-24-18+13

16-61-12-26-11+16   4-14-18-40-33+15

41-15-5-25-26+4   52-30-16-38-50+15

69-54-57-46-45+16   61-57-15-58-26+19

66-1-64-11-58+15   58-43-35-40-4+2

48-35-30-55-11+3   37-40-3-20-43+24

21-61-25-12-60+21   34-52-44-46-59+20

62-33-20-31-24+10   55-26-66-28-5+25

5-24-22-1-68+23   42-29-24-2-16+12

42-29-18-15-56+17   42-31-25-59-60+19

Xchange judgment for understanding; empathy bridges divides.	Xpectations are like chains; break free and live authentically.
Xemplify kindness in all your interactions; it leaves a lasting impression.	Xpectations are the seeds of disappointment; embrace acceptance instead.
Xemplify resilience in the face of adversity; you are stronger than you know.	Xpectations limit potential; release them and embrace the flow of life.
Xercise your creativity daily; it's a muscle that grows with use.	Xperience the beauty of simplicity; it brings clarity and peace.
Xhale deeply and release tension; peace resides in each breath.	Xperience the joy of giving without expecting anything in return.
Xhilarate your mind with learning and discovery; knowledge is liberation.	Xperience the present moment fully; it's where true happiness resides.
Xhilarate your senses by immersing yourself in nature's beauty.	Xplore the depths of your imagination; it holds limitless potential.
Xhilarate your spirit with laughter; it's the best medicine.	Xplore the depths of your soul; therein lies infinite wisdom.
Xpand your awareness to include the interconnectedness of all things.	Xplore the power of forgiveness; it frees you from the past.
Xpand your circle of compassion to include all beings; we are interconnected.	Xplore the unknown with curiosity and courage; therein lies growth and transformation.
Xpand your comfort zone; growth happens on the edge.	Xplore the world with wonder and curiosity; it's a playground of possibilities.
Xpand your horizons by embracing diversity and difference.	Xpress gratitude for the abundance in your life; it attracts more blessings.
Xpect miracles in the most unexpected places; keep your heart open.	Xpress your love freely; it's the greatest gift you can give.

22-61-3-22-51+9   13-10-53-25-62+22

50-43-56-66-6+1   68-62-2-60-65+24

45-21-58-50-63+4   69-4-34-31-55+21

47-11-42-15-33+18   38-22-19-11-64+16

9-22-10-23-37+5   56-13-69-36-22+3

37-10-3-49-8+17   61-59-43-49-11+5

50-14-48-24-5+10   45-7-60-21-47+6

4-20-7-6-15+13   51-30-14-11-52+19

15-14-54-20-55+22   59-33-63-20-15+11

40-42-58-37-34+13   30-17-23-16-13+3

19-60-40-10-69+21   5-50-51-69-62+21

39-64-4-41-42+14   62-48-15-4-63+15

43-33-20-54-58+9   2-27-19-21-8+4

Xtraordinary opportunities await those who dare to dream big.	Yearn for simplicity in a world of complexity; it brings clarity.
Yearn for adventure and embrace the unknown; it's where growth thrives.	Yearn for understanding and empathy; they foster compassion.
Yearn for authenticity in a world of masks; it is the truest expression of self.	Yield not to complacency, but to the drive for continuous improvement.
Yearn for balance in all things; it is the path to harmony.	Yield not to despair, for every challenge is an opportunity in disguise.
Yearn for connection with others; it is the fabric of humanity.	Yield not to doubt, but to the belief in your own abilities.
Yearn for connection with your true self; it holds the answers you seek.	Yield not to fear, but let courage be your guide.
Yearn for fulfillment in all areas of your life; you deserve nothing less.	Yield not to negativity, but to the light within you.
Yearn for growth and evolution; change is the only constant.	Yield not to temptation, but to the strength of your character.
Yearn for inner peace; it is found in the stillness of your soul.	Yield to the call of adventure; it beckons you to new heights.
Yearn for knowledge and wisdom; they are the keys to enlightenment.	Yield to the flow of creativity; it is the essence of your being.
Yearn for laughter and joy; they are the elixirs of life.	Yield to the power of forgiveness; it sets you free from the past.
Yearn for progress, not perfection; it is the journey that matters most.	Yield to the power of gratitude; it unlocks the abundance of the universe.
Yearn for resilience in the face of adversity; it builds character.	Yield to the power of love; it heals, transforms, and unites.

7-33-39-62-35+7   36-8-62-22-50+7

45-22-61-9-43+10   9-15-35-34-43+8

69-53-48-69-38+12   40-61-46-23-55+12

20-30-32-5-7+16   69-5-59-8-28+6

32-64-25-47-20+2   64-26-29-50-21+12

18-65-4-14-12+9   41-48-15-63-4+14

56-15-46-66-68+23   7-68-23-22-10+18

69-34-36-67-58+19   56-14-61-58-42+18

63-34-6-69-5+8   68-8-5-58-15+9

18-8-3-29-9+9   56-53-23-19-44+6

15-1-30-48-38+13   61-6-25-29-66+15

30-24-43-53-2+14   32-35-34-53-49+3

51-5-1-52-7+18   57-62-39-69-17+22

Yield to the rhythm of life; there is beauty in its ebb and flow.	You are a traveler at heart. You'll take many journeys.
Yield to the wisdom of experience; it is a beacon in the darkness.	You are a wonderful human being.
Yield to the wisdom of nature; it holds the secrets of life.	You are able to undertake and accomplish anything.
Yoke your dreams to action; they are the seeds of your destiny.	You are about to embark on a delightful journey.
Yonder lies your dreams; pursue them with passion and perseverance.	You are almost there.
You achieve great peace of mind when you talk with an old friend.	You are capable of fulfilling your ambitions.
You are a good listener.	You are capable, competent, creative, and careful. Prove it.
You are a lover of words, someday you will write a book.	You are careful and systematic in your business arrangements.
You are a person of another time.	You are cautious in showing your true self to others.
You are a person of righteousness and integrity.	You are generous to an extreme and always think of others.
You are a practical person with your feet on the ground.	You are going to have some new clothes.
You are a source of wisdom and strength to many people.	You are going to take a vacation.
You are a talented storyteller.	You are humorous and cheerful with good friends.

52-28-45-65-43+3   68-42-54-60-3+23

11-21-51-39-30+3   37-69-56-4-58+6

41-64-15-54-29+3   62-16-36-22-62+5

21-47-10-58-35+3   26-21-60-49-8+1

56-50-37-33-53+13   27-8-57-19-36+1

11-9-52-42-13+9   61-30-6-39-64+9

40-46-42-5-24+17   2-34-56-29-45+2

45-40-49-6-50+20   42-54-60-44-60+25

56-45-26-66-6+25   50-25-26-1-5+10

40-21-4-3-58+2   50-60-8-39-47+24

69-14-6-11-24+17   38-25-27-57-58+10

32-16-45-69-20+21   18-52-22-17-61+6

23-40-41-9-25+8   34-57-18-30-7+11

You are imbued with extraordinary vitality.	You are solid and dependable.
You are in for an enlightening experience.	You are talented in many ways.
You are in good hands this evening.	You are the center of every group's attention.
You are known for being quick in action and decisions.	You are the controller of your destiny.
You are more likely to give than give in.	You are the greatest person in the world.
You are never selfish with your advice or your help.	You are the master of every situation.
You are next in line for promotion in your job.	You are very expressive and positive in words, acts and feelings.
You are not a person who can be ignored.	You are very grateful for the small pleasures of life.
You are offered the dream of a lifetime. Say yes!	You can always find happiness at work on Monday.
You are on your way.	You can be trusted to keep a secret.
You are open-minded and quick to make new friends.	You can have your cake and eat it too, so stop whining.
You are perceptive and considerate when dealing with others.	You can not get to the top by sitting on your bottom.
You are sociable and entertaining.	You cannot push a cow's head down unless it is drinking water by its own will.

51-6-52-50-42+22   50-30-41-55-45+9

14-50-31-21-51+9   14-32-48-53-57+4

32-5-35-19-9+25   39-36-55-66-68+10

42-38-22-36-47+25   3-44-30-22-28+14

65-57-39-36-44+9   8-21-18-48-34+2

56-35-40-49-43+14   52-4-44-15-69+20

4-22-18-44-29+7   15-7-68-41-50+7

33-2-31-5-29+2   1-1-25-63-37+2

60-3-63-14-24+21   14-69-57-58-65+17

46-66-53-61-57+1   56-57-2-54-68+9

13-31-33-29-9+5   47-24-46-36-38+19

46-16-33-31-27+10   58-64-3-10-38+22

17-15-25-69-13+13   28-21-8-29-49+24

You create enthusiasm around you.	You have an unusually magnetic personality.
You display the wonderful traits of charm and courtesy.	You have exceeded what was expected.
You do not hesitate to tackle the most difficult problems.	You have tasted both the bitterness and sweetness of coffee.
You have a deep appreciation of the arts and music.	You have the ability to touch the lives of many people.
You have a deep interest in all that is artistic.	You have the power to write your own fortune.
You have a fine capacity for the enjoyment of life.	You have the rare ability to decide quickly and wisely.
You have a great personality and a burning ambition to succeed.	You have unusual equipment for success, use it properly.
You have a pair of shining eyes.	You have yearning for perfection.
You have a quiet and unobtrusive nature.	You long to see the great pyramids in Egypt.
You have a shrewd knack for spotting insincerity.	You love the thrill of showmanship and display.
You have an active mind and a keen imagination.	You maintain a sense of balance in the midst of great success.
You have an ambitious nature and will make a name for yourself.	You make people realize that there exist other beauties in the world.
You have an important new business development shaping up.	You may have to be patient now– think, listen and heed signs.

41-54-31-49-65+7   18-49-16-2-65+17

10-67-22-4-67+14   32-39-26-5-2+12

64-6-36-38-7+14   9-15-59-51-27+25

57-37-28-35-36+5   18-13-55-69-57+22

35-65-24-44-52+5   27-62-51-53-31+21

35-45-22-68-15+9   9-40-52-69-58+7

8-3-16-4-38+17   2-18-46-69-20+12

4-62-47-15-5+21   11-21-40-18-54+7

60-5-33-62-21+9   11-68-51-27-29+2

43-56-45-33-55+21   20-57-56-54-22+21

67-4-33-7-37+2   22-55-58-14-33+2

1-49-14-37-60+6   22-5-9-2-58+23

27-49-16-57-60+12   31-2-41-22-59+5

You need not worry about your future.	You understand how to have fun with others, and to enjoy your solitude.
You never hesitate to tackle the most difficult problems.	You want your horse to look good but you also want it not to have to eat grass.
You seek to shield those you love and like the role of protector.	You will advance the careers of your friends in your climb to success.
You shall soon achieve perfection.	You will always be surrounded by true friends.
You share a true and sincere friendship.	You will always have good luck in your personal affairs.
You should be able to undertake and complete anything you desire.	You will always possess a charm and sense of humor that attracts others.
You should be of more tenderness and less aggressiveness.	You will attend an unusual party.
You should have a talk with a friend today.	You will attract cultured and artistic people to your home.
You show your true face to the people who really matter.	You will be a great success both in the business world and society.
You simplify your life in many ways and find great rewards.	You will be advanced socially without any special effort.
You stand in your own light. Make it shIne.	You will be attracted to an older, more experienced person.
You take a reverent attitude toward life and are most capable in the guidance of others.	You will be called upon to help a friend in trouble.
You think that it is a secret, but it never has been one.	You will be fortunate in everything you put your hands to.

1-40-63-51-44+6

22-62-3-32-42+14

22-39-18-3-21+17

21-33-30-62-2+7

21-9-10-60-65+7

67-34-69-44-54+14

37-30-6-5-63+15

52-67-42-58-61+19

48-1-54-28-17+10

13-21-28-41-39+11

17-53-2-25-53+16

38-7-53-45-55+8

18-22-23-32-45+11

24-19-15-68-20+11

51-55-2-69-33+17

31-44-11-8-54+17

31-59-44-14-56+21

30-14-1-16-48+18

22-44-38-52-69+9

64-65-48-47-48+9

8-35-11-54-40+12

24-59-69-22-47+12

50-36-24-17-67+11

57-42-38-46-25+4

25-40-56-39-37+20

45-44-38-20-53+4

You will be happy and recipient of Good News.	You will find a real bargain.
You will be rewarded with great honor.	You will find money or gold.
You will be selected for a promotion because of your accomplishments.	You will find what you're looking for; just open your eyes!
You will be sought out for your diplomatic skills.	You will have a close encounter of a serious kind.
You will be spending time outdoors, in the mountains, near water.	You will have a long and prosperous life.
You will be successful in your work.	You will have a sudden change for the better.
You will be traveling and coming into a fortune.	You will have gold pieces by the bushel.
You will be unusually successful in business.	You will have many important meetings, visits, and chance encounters.
You will become a great philanthropist in your later years.	You will have the attention of those you encounter.
You will conquer all obstacles and achieve success.	You will inherit a large sum of money.
You will emerge from uncertainty into great peace and freedom.	You will inherit some money or a small piece of land.
You will enjoy good health that is your form of wealth.	You will make a change for the better.
You will fall in love.	You will make many changes before settling down happily.

31-65-34-37-39+23	36-15-27-21-39+21
12-45-7-25-24+6	63-4-53-39-60+3
63-41-10-31-50+12	69-34-9-7-18+9
60-69-4-68-2+8	3-61-32-27-24+7
22-52-28-36-67+4	28-52-29-65-61+5
34-49-57-30-31+15	34-38-62-45-48+19
69-28-10-16-48+7	35-53-35-52-6+12
19-23-65-27-25+12	68-7-21-23-65+8
68-51-17-54-45+7	8-65-13-63-30+21
68-21-66-23-22+12	22-64-44-21-31+21
56-30-18-37-10+9	8-43-35-26-20+12
50-5-42-21-25+5	4-39-41-7-11+14
18-61-44-58-15+21	68-25-30-62-65+1

You will meet an important person who will help you advance professionally.	Your abilities are unparalleled.
You will never regret the present; you live life to the fullest!	Your ability is appreciated.
You will receive many beauteous gifts in the years ahead.	Your ability to accomplish matters will follow with success.
You will see through the illusion to the plain truth.	Your ability to find the silly in the serious will take you far!
You will show what you are capable of.	Your ability to juggle many tasks will take you far.
You will soon be honored by someone you respect.	Your artistic talents win the approval and applause of others.
You will spend old age in comfort and material wealth.	Your biggest virtue is your modesty.
You will succeed through your charm and personality.	Your boss will soon learn to appreciate you.
You will take a chance on something in the near future.	Your co-workers take pleasure in your great sense of creativity!
You will take a pleasant journey to a place far away.	Your determination will bring you much success.
You will travel far and wide for both pleasure and business.	Your difficulties will strengthen you.
You're beginning to appreciate how important it is to share your personal beliefs.	Your dreams are never silly; depend on them to guide you.
You're transforming yourself into someone who is certain to succeed.	Your dreams are worth your best efforts to achieve them.

12-60-13-22-30+18

30-2-69-40-53+20

68-53-48-4-67+21

30-63-35-20-46+4

48-36-26-64-15+22

32-44-20-14-59+20

42-37-12-21-59+18

43-29-22-8-43+21

51-67-46-53-13+7

47-67-22-36-11+15

11-40-69-52-26+2

23-30-26-36-3+1

35-4-51-69-59+24

3-60-11-39-49+13

13-23-34-9-53+13

69-65-17-48-1+15

11-58-4-16-59+18

28-45-6-19-15+12

34-47-5-23-26+20

66-6-2-35-5+16

55-23-15-20-65+2

62-48-22-33-26+7

41-58-69-7-59+22

37-39-68-46-20+1

17-58-8-20-29+11

19-45-46-8-51+7

- Your emotional nature is strong and sensitive.
- Your home is the center of great love.
- Your example will inspire others.
- Your ideals are well within your reach.
- Your excellent memory coupled with your effervescent charm will lead you to success.
- Your ingenuity and imagination will get results.
- Your first love has never forgotten you.
- Your kindness is surely to be repaid.
- Your future is as boundless as the lofty heavens.
- Your know it all approach will soon pay off.
- Your future is sweet.
- Your leadership qualities will be tested and proven.
- Your future will be happy and productive.
- Your life becomes more and more of an adventure!
- Your good deeds are never forgotten.
- Your life will be happy and peaceful.
- Your greatest fortune is the large number of friends you have.
- Your life will get more and more exciting.
- Your happiness is intertwined with your outlook on life.
- Your love of life will carry you through any circumstance.
- Your heart is a place to draw true happiness.
- Your love of music is an important part of your life.
- Your heart will always make itself known through your words.
- Your love will be happy and harmonious.
- Your home is a pleasant place from which you draw happiness.
- Your luck has completely changed today.

9-53-24-41-30+17   58-35-56-42-18+19

7-35-47-51-24+16   6-13-21-43-10+9

20-39-56-17-47+23   9-37-16-41-62+25

12-11-59-26-41+20   51-17-45-36-6+7

28-31-12-39-65+9   28-9-41-15-14+15

51-16-61-36-15+12   18-24-59-15-5+4

69-51-17-31-27+18   33-54-69-26-58+10

7-13-44-52-18+9   23-68-24-33-15+23

3-35-39-17-9+19   23-6-36-69-55+7

43-2-61-48-2+18   38-24-37-53-57+17

43-30-25-23-5+2   47-56-63-62-22+21

42-47-34-43-29+14   42-28-50-30-27+6

52-61-47-69-13+20   60-61-10-46-48+1

Your many hidden talents will become obvious to those around you.	Your spirit of adventure leads you down an exciting new path.
Your mind is your greatest asset.	Your success will astonish everyone.
Your objective is difficult but worth it.	Your sweetheart may be too beautiful for words, but not for arguments.
Your past success will be overshadowed by your future success.	Your talents will be recognized and suitably rewarded.
Your personal finances will greatly improve.	Your uniqueness is more than an outward experience.
Your present plans are going to succeed.	Your virtues are your priceless treasures.
Your quick wits will get you out of a tough situation.	Your work interests can capture the highest status or prestige.
Your reputation is your wealth.	Zeal for kindness spreads like wildfire; ignite it with your actions.
Your secret desire to completely change your life will succeed.	Zeal for life's adventures makes every moment an opportunity; seize it with gusto.
Your sense of humor reveals itself at just the right times!	Zeal is the fuel for achievement; let it ignite your actions.
Your skills and talents will be called on in unusual areas.	Zealously chase your dreams; they are waiting to be realized.
Your skills will accomplish what the force of many cannot.	Zealously embrace change; it's the only constant in life.
Your smile makes everyone realize that the world is a lovely and beautiful place.	Zealously protect your dreams from doubt and negativity; they are precious.

23-2-41-58-28+17					11-42-55-2-51+5

3-23-44-30-50+2					27-55-62-15-37+10

12-64-10-47-33+20					39-2-10-47-45+23

22-1-63-19-53+9					45-51-12-46-6+16

62-13-69-41-61+3					8-50-55-34-37+7

65-30-39-51-28+12					33-36-13-29-52+21

44-7-13-18-67+8					34-59-12-9-10+8

27-2-57-35-60+24					21-31-55-42-26+6

43-42-65-26-60+20					27-18-16-41-3+8

67-13-31-6-19+8					23-69-37-10-19+16

47-17-16-30-39+9					62-54-64-9-26+10

10-27-39-35-29+23					28-53-48-68-51+22

49-34-37-59-22+5					28-11-29-30-5+20

Zealously pursue personal growth; it's the path to self-realization.	Zero in on what truly matters in life; let go of distractions.
Zealously pursue your dreams; they are the seeds of your future.	Zero in on your goals and pursue them with unwavering determination.
Zen attitude cultivates tranquility amidst chaos; find your inner calm.	Zest for adventure leads to unforgettable experiences; dare to explore.
Zen gardens teach the art of tranquility; cultivate inner peace.	Zest for challenges fuels growth and resilience; face them boldly.
Zen is found in the present moment; let go of worries about the past and future.	Zest for creativity fuels innovation and ingenuity; let it flow freely.
Zen moments are found in the simplest of pleasures; savor them fully.	Zest for learning opens doors to endless possibilities; keep exploring.
Zen philosophy teaches the art of letting go; release what no longer serves you.	Zest for life is contagious; sprinkle it everywhere you go.
Zen-like acceptance brings peace amidst turbulence; surrender and find serenity.	Zestful living means embracing each day with enthusiasm and gratitude.
Zen-like calmness in chaos is a superpower; cultivate it within.	Zigzßag through life's twists and turns with resilience and grace.
Zeniths are reached one step at a time; keep climbing towards your aspirations.	Zoom into your passions and let them guide you towards fulfillment.
Zephyrs of change bring renewal and transformation; embrace them with openness.	Zoom out and gain perspective; life's challenges are part of a bigger picture.
Zephyrs of change whisper softly; listen closely and be ready to adapt.	Zoom into your soul and grab the last ounce of strength until you reach your goal.
Zephyrs of inspiration whisper softly; be attuned to their guidance.	Zoom out and gain wisdom in every day challenges.

19-45-40-63-2+2

20-69-7-66-5+8

41-43-15-17-49+13

13-47-17-6-8+9

60-48-58-50-19+20

15-42-67-24-40+9

1-61-34-54-2+12

35-53-14-60-6+20

31-48-64-65-23+22

9-45-24-32-7+3

26-69-48-18-4+4

63-68-58-6-21+12

53-60-29-27-31+19

22-16-57-13-2+15

14-54-18-15-66+2

33-59-65-35-37+21

69-26-46-15-37+13

9-43-13-25-28+6

47-40-7-37-67+15

54-10-47-33-4+17

63-27-28-32-39+1

58-13-54-61-63+24

50-28-23-63-42+22

59-34-60-43-36+10

61-46-57-40-29+2

10-56-50-45-17+23

www.ingramcontent.com/pod-product-compliance
Lightning Source LLC
LaVergne TN
LVHW051657080426
835511LV00017B/2616